LAIKOS

Laymen
Lay People
Lay Pastors
Volunteers

DAG HEWARD-MILLS

Parchment House

First published 2013 by Parchment House
5th Printing 2014

Find out more about Dag Heward-Mills at:

Healing Jesus Campaign
Write to: evangelist@daghewardmills.org
Website: www.daghewardmills.org
Facebook: Dag Heward-Mills
Twitter: @EvangelistDag

ISBN: 978-9988-8552-9-1

Contents

Chapter 1

LAIKOS: The Layman

[handwritten: lack of skills]

The word layman comes from the Greek word LAIKOS which means "having no skills". History teaches us that great things can be accomplished through people who "lack skills". A quick glance at the achievements of lay people or common people will inspire you to use them in the ministry. Through laymen, souls will be saved, cells will be established, churches will grow and God's work will flourish.

The following are a few definitions of the word layman:

1. A layman is an ordinary person.
2. A layman is a normal person.
3. A layman is a commonplace person.
4. A layman is a usual person.
5. A layman is a regular person.
6. A layman is a common person.
7. A layman is an everyday person.
8. A layman is an average person.
9. A layman is someone who is not a professional.
10. A layman is someone who is not an expert.
11. A layman is someone who is not specialized.
12. A layman is someone who is not skilled.
13. A layman is someone who is not trained.
14. A layman is someone who is not certified.
15. A layman is someone who is not licensed.

Great Achievements in the Church World

1. Lay people were the pillars of the great reformation of the church.

Martin Luther's translation of the Bible into the language of the common people changed the world. Instead of just being in Latin, the Bible was made more accessible to the common people. Once the common/lay people had revelation knowledge in their hands they changed the world. Realising that salvation was available to all men through the grace of God they rose up and championed what we now know as the Reformation.

2. Lay people are the pillars of the great Methodist Church.

By the middle of the 20th century, Methodism was the largest Protestant denomination in the United States. The great Methodist church has ridden on the backs of lay people.

A very early tradition of preaching in the Methodist churches was for a Lay Preacher to be appointed to lead services of worship and preach in a group of churches called a "circuit".

The lay preacher walked or rode on horseback in a prescribed circuit of the preaching places according to an agreed pattern and timing.

After the appointment of ministers and pastors, this lay preaching tradition continued with ''Methodist Local Preachers'' being appointed by individual churches, and in turn approved and invited by nearby churches, as an adjunct to the minister or during their planned absences.

3. Lay people were the pillars of the largest single church in the world.

One of the foundational principles on which the Yoido Full Gospel Church is built is the principle of working through lay people.

The Yoido Full Gospel Church, founded by David Yonggi Cho and his mother-in-law, Choi Ja-shil, both Assemblies of God pastors, held its maiden worship service on May 15, 1958 with four other ladies in the home of Choi Ja-shil.

Membership of the church had reached fifty thousand by 1977, a figure that doubled in only two years. On 30 November 1981, membership topped two hundred thousand. By this time, it was the largest single congregation in the world and was recognized as such by the Los Angeles Times.

In 2007 its membership stood at 830,000, with seven Sunday services translated into sixteen languages.

4. **Lay people are the pillars of huge networks of churches originating from Nigeria and Ghana.**

Both the Redeemed Christian Church of God with its home in Nigeria and The Church of Pentecost with its headquarters in Ghana are known to make good use of lay people. Both of these ministries have huge networks of churches and regularly employ the services of lay people for preaching and pastoring.

The Church of Pentecost was founded by James McKeon, an Irish missionary sent by the Apostolic Church, Bradford, UK to the then Gold Coast.

It has grown to have a membership of over 1.7 million members. The Church of Pentecost has over 13,000 churches in 70 countries across all the continents of the world.

In 1952, Pa Josiah Akindayomi founded the Redeemed Christian Church of God in Nigeria.

Under the leadership of its General Overseer, Reverend E.A. Adeboye, it has grown to have churches in more than 140 countries, with millions in attendance.

Truly, these are great achievements and they have been made possible through the inputs of lay people.

Great Achievements in the Secular World

1. **The great government system of democracy was birthed through lay people.**

Democracy is giving common people the opportunity to act and change the government if they wish.

Democracy is the common man's power to refuse to live under unacceptable conditions.

Democracy is the common man's participation and influence in a country.

Democracy is built upon the principle of equal opportunity given to all common people.

2. The great super-power was given birth to through lay people.

The American Revolution is a classic example of the power of the common or lay people in shaping history. The common man gave birth to a superpower. At the turn of the last century, the American Revolution was a successful experiment that marked the transition of a world controlled by a few to a world controlled by the many.

The Revolution was largely shaped by small revolutionary organizations such as the Sons of Liberty. These organizations were not controlled by the rich and powerful landowners but common people of average social status came together to plant the seeds of the Revolution.

3. The historic election victory of Barack Obama came through lay people.

In May 2008, Barack Obama, first black president of the United States of America, clinched the Democratic nomination for the presidency of the United States.

Even though the country's rich and influential Democrats were Clinton supporters and provided the millions of dollars, Obama raised more than any other presidential candidate in history by using the power of the common person.

Obama raised over $80 million in his campaign, most of which came from common people making small individual contributions.

Chapter 2

What Happens When There Are No Laymen and Volunteers

1. **If you do not allow volunteers to work in the ministry you will kill the Christian principle of sacrifice in the church.**

   Then said Jesus unto his disciples, If any man will come after me, let him deny himself, and take up his cross, and follow me.

   Matthew 16:24

The symbol of Christianity is the cross. The cross speaks of suffering and dying. God spoke to Abraham and asked him to give up his most treasured possession - his son. Don't listen to anyone who tells you that the day of suffering, sacrificing, losing and dying is over. The day of suffering, sacrificing, losing and dying has come! God is requiring us to give up our treasured possessions so that we can serve Him. The church is being filled with people who are not aware that God is calling them to sacrifice. Christianity is a religion of sacrifice. Christianity is based on the cross. Christianity is based on losing your life so that you gain a new life.

Different Sacrifices for Different People

But some people have the mistaken view that God asks everyone to sacrifice their "Isaac". But God did not ask Joseph to sacrifice his sons. Neither did He ask Jacob or Isaac to sacrifice their sons. King David was a man after God's own heart, but God did not ask David to sacrifice his son.

God deals with everyone differently! What God requires of me may be different from what He requires of you. God has asked me for my profession. Perhaps God will not ask you for your profession. *But He will ask you for something and you will have to give it up.*

5

Christianity always involves sacrifice. If you do not allow lay people to work in the ministry, they will never learn to give up the smallest things for Christ. If they cannot give up their time, their evenings and their leisure for Christ what will happen if the Lord asks them for their "Isaac"? It is important to expose the lay people in your church to this basic principle of sacrifice.

2. If you do not allow laymen to work in the ministry you will remove the opportunity for people to demonstrate faithfulness.

The Bible teaches clearly that he that is faithful with little will be faithful with much.

He that is faithful in that which is least is faithful also in much: and he that is unjust in the least is unjust also in much. If therefore ye have not been faithful in the unrighteous mammon, who will commit to your trust the true riches? And if ye have not been faithful in that which is another man's, who shall give you that which is your own?

Luke 16:10-12

If somebody is not faithful as a layperson, how will he be faithful when he is in full-time ministry? Many people do not do well in full-time ministry because they did not do well as lay people.

Did you work for the Lord as a layperson who did not need supervision? Did you need anybody to tell you to get up to pray? Did you need anybody to tell you to study your Bible? Were you faithful when you were in school?

I was a committed worker in the Scripture Union fellowship in my school. I was heavily involved as an organist in a Christian singing group to which I belonged. I was a drummer and pianist for Victory Church in London. I was involved with the fellowships in the university. Yet it never once crossed my mind that I should be paid for these things.

This lay ministry is an important background for a future full-time ministry.

He that is faithful with lay ministry will be faithful with full-time ministry. Many people who have worked as lay people work even better as full-timers.

3. If you do not allow lay people to work in the ministry you will employ people to do jobs that do not occupy them fully.

Not every ministry needs a full-time pastor. Many churches can be pastored by unpaid lay pastors.

If there are only twenty-five people in the church, it is obvious that it cannot sustain and does not need a full-time minister. Many of the church members secretly ask, "What does the full-time pastor do all day?"

Many people think that pastors sleep from morning to evening. The fact is that there isn't so much to do with a congregation of thirty. The ministry has to develop to the point where it needs a full-time worker. The other reality is that most of the members are at work during the day and only become available in the evenings.

Pastors are not bankers, accountants or pharmacists. They are shepherds who are supposed to look after sheep. Working hours are different for different professions! I do not work from nine to five every day because I am not an accountant. I am a pastor! When the sheep become available in the evenings I become very active. That is why I work late into the night.

Some pastors become idle and lazy as they wait for Sunday when they can deliver their next sermon.

For we hear that there are some which walk among you disorderly, WORKING NOT AT ALL...

2 Thessalonians 3:11

Let us be honest! Let us be realistic! Does your church need so many full-time pastors? Does it need even one full-time pastor? Can the income of the church sustain the pastor and his family? Can the pastor not find a secular job to do? Pastors are frustrated and fearful because they are not sure whether they will be able to survive until the next month.

You can overcome that frustration today! Get a job and pastor the church on the side until it grows and demands your full attention!

The Swiss missionaries who were sent to Ghana many years ago were sent as *self-sustaining ministers*. They came equipped with skills that would enable them to work in Africa as they did their ministry work. That is a good example to follow. We need self-sustaining ministers today more than ever before. Most churches cannot bear the burden of maintaining so many full-time pastors.

You must keep your ministry staff as small as possible so that you can pay them properly. You must not have idle and discontented people around you. Idleness leads to laziness and laziness leads to discontentment and discontentment leads to disloyalty.

And withal they learn to be idle, wandering about from house to house; and not only idle, but tattlers also and busybodies, speaking things which they ought not.

1 Timothy 5:13

4. If you do not allow volunteers to work in the ministry everything done in the church will be related to money.

He that loveth silver shall not be satisfied with silver; nor he that loveth abundance with increase: this is also vanity.

Ecclesiastes 5:10

The ministry is not an alternative source of employment for anyone. It was never intended to be! It is a special job that God gives to those whom He has called. **As the church becomes**

larger, it often deteriorates into a source of employment for the unemployed. This attracts many people who have no better options. What happens to the church? It becomes full of seekers of wealth and lovers of silver. The church is filled with pastors who constantly fight for better salaries and conditions of service.

I started ministry as a layperson, so the idea of being paid in full-time ministry came up much later. I started my church as a medical student and found myself pastoring while at the same time practising medicine. Later on, I went into business and combined it with pastoral work.

At the end of 1990, the Lord told me to leave everything I was doing and enter into full-time ministry. It was not an easy decision for me. Since January 1st, 1991 I have been full-time in the ministry for the Lord Jesus.

There are many people who are in full-time ministry who should not really be there. There are many people who I believe should find secular jobs! How can a church with sixty members sustain eight full-time pastors and their families? Yet, this is the case in many ministries. Success in the ministry requires both power and wisdom.

But unto them which are called, both Jews and Greeks, Christ the power of God, and the wisdom of God.

1 Corinthians 1:24

Many pastors see the ministry as a way to travel around the world and to drive nice cars. I did not enter the ministry in order to drive a nice car. I do drive a nice car now but I did not come into the ministry because I wanted to have the nice things of this world. In fact, coming into full-time ministry was, for me, the end of all hopes of ever having the nice things of this world.

Yea doubtless, and I count all things but loss for the excellency of the knowledge of Christ Jesus my Lord: for whom I HAVE SUFFERED THE LOSS OF ALL THINGS, and do count them but dung, that I may win Christ,

Philippians 3:8

A minister who is going to serve God properly must have died to the love for silver and gold. Why is this? The Bible teaches that those that love silver are never satisfied with silver. The more you give them, the more they want. Why is it that the richest people in this world are often the biggest thieves? Is it because they are poor? Is it because they are in need? Certainly not! It is because of the greed for more and more and more!

You cannot satisfy people who want more and more money. From experience, whenever I have felt under pressure to raise salaries, I have often discovered it does not solve the problem!

Senior pastors, if you feel under pressure to raise salaries and give more and more benefits, you will discover that the problem never goes away. Full-time ministers must be people who just want to serve the Lord at heart. This does not mean that people will be poor but it means that the heart is not craving endlessly after more and more.

Soon the church becomes unionized with the workers against the management, and the management against the workers! The "management" are often the senior pastors who make decisions and the "workers" are the other pastors and workers who are not involved in the decision-making. You should see the bitterness, petty jealousies and bickering amongst the full-time staff of many churches and ministries. This often extends to their families and pastor's wives pick up quarrels with other pastor's wives.

I would rather have one or two workers with peace than to have a hundred unhappy and discontented full-time staff.

5. If you do not allow laymen to work in the ministry people will not learn obedience and submission.

As you enter into full-time ministry you must be open for whatever the future will bring. You may be rich or you may be poor. You may have abundance or you may live in the "want of all things". Are you ready for anything?

Verily, verily, I say unto thee, When thou wast young, thou girdedst thyself, and walkedst whither thou wouldest: but when thou shalt be old, thou shalt stretch forth thy hands, and another shall gird thee, and carry thee whither thou wouldest not.

This spake he, signifying by what death he should glorify God. And when he had spoken this, he saith unto him, Follow me.

John 21:18-19

Jesus told Peter to be ready for anything. Be ready to be carried anywhere. It will no longer be your will, but God's will. You are not the commander, you are just one of God's workers. One of the reasons why I am in the ministry is because I have no choice.

...woe is unto me, if I preach not the gospel!

1 Corinthians 9:16

There are detractors, faultfinders, analysts and commentators who talk about me all the time. I have no time for empty chatter. I prefer to hear my dogs barking in the morning than to listen to their hateful and sarcastic comments. I must continue doing what God has called me to do. Some people love me for what I do and others hate me. I thank God for them all. But I press on for the mark of the prize of the high calling.

I am totally surrendered to fulfilling the call of God upon my life, so help me God!

Chapter 3

Seven Reasons Why God Operates through Lay People

All through the Scriptures, you see God giving different gifts to different people. To some He gives one talent and to others He gives many talents. I believe that it is the ministry of the one talent. However, it is important to value this ministry even if it is only one talent. Your judgment for despising the one talent will be severe.

Why do I call it the ministry of one talent? Those in full-time ministry give all their days, nights, weeks and months to the Lord's work whilst those who are volunteers may give one day in the week for this ministry. You cannot compare the output and the sacrifice of a one-evening-a-week ministry with that of a hundred per cent full-time dedicated ministry. Does that mean that the lay ministry is not valid? Not at all! Some people have been called by the Holy Spirit to work for God with one talent. "But all these worketh that one and the selfsame Spirit, dividing to every man severally as he will" (1Corinthians 12:11).

It is the will of God that some people have one talent while some have ten. It is the will of God that some people work for God once a week whilst others work for Him every day. Your judgment will be based on your faithfulness to your mission and your call.

Why God Operates through Lay People

1. **The gift of ministry is *measured.*** Some people receive a larger measure than others. That is the will of God.

   For I say, through the grace given unto me, to every man that is among you, not to think of himself more highly than he ought to think; but to think soberly, according as GOD

HATH DEALT TO EVERY MAN THE MEASURE OF FAITH.

Romans 12:3

2. **God has decided to give everyone** *a different office.* Some have the office of the all-out minister working full time. Others are given the office of a lay person.

For as we have many members in one body, and ALL MEMBERS HAVE NOT THE SAME OFFICE:

Romans 12:4

3. **God gives some people** *only one talent.* You cannot ask God why He gives some people only one talent. That is His decision. Those with only one talent are able to work for the Lord in a much smaller capacity.

For the kingdom of heaven is as a man travelling into a far country, who called his own servants, and delivered unto them his goods and UNTO ONE HE GAVE FIVE TALENTS, TO ANOTHER TWO, AND TO ANOTHER ONE; To every man according to his several ability; and straightway took his journey.

Matthew 25:14-15

4. **Some people** *do not have the ability* **for full-time ministry.** If you force people who do not have the divine ability to be in full-time ministry, you will only create rebels and spiritual tragedies. Accept the reality that everyone has been given different abilities by the Lord.

For the kingdom of heaven is as a man travelling into a far country, who called his own servants, and delivered unto them his goods and unto one he gave five talents, to another two, and to another one; to every man ACCORDING TO HIS SEVERAL ABILITY; and straightway took his journey.

Matthew 25:14-15

5. **The *Holy Spirit works* through all ministries no matter how diverse they are.** This is why the lay ministry can be as anointed as full-time ministry. That is why the contribution of lay ministers and volunteers can be as powerful and meaningful as a full-time minister. The Holy Spirit works through the lay ministry just as much as He does through the full-time ministry. There are many Spirit-anointed laymen who walk in God's wonderful calling.

    But ALL THESE WORKETH THAT ONE AND THE SELFSAME SPIRIT, dividing to every man severally as he will.

    1 Corinthians 12:11

6. **God *administers* His power in different ways.** God Almighty can administer His love for mankind through a layman.

    And there are DIFFERENCES OF ADMINISTRATIONS, but the same Lord.

    1 Corinthians 12:5

7. **God *operates* in different ways. God Almighty can operate through a volunteer.** Who can question God's operations?

    And there are DIVERSITIES OF OPERATIONS, but it is the same God which worketh all in all.

    1 Corinthians 12:6

Chapter 4

Seven Things You Must Know about the Lay Ministry

1. The Lay ministry will greatly enhance the work of church planting.

One of the greatest keys to extensive church planting is the lay ministry. The lay ministry is the sacrifice of pastors and evangelists, who labour without being paid for their services. The enormity of the work is such that, without the strategy of lay ministry, very few churches will be planted. Almost every ministry I know has ground to a halt because of mounting bills, and the high cost of maintaining staff. It is virtually IMPOSSIBLE for the church to employ the people that are needed for the work of God.

The lay ministry is not popular in some circles. In some cultures everybody must be paid for his services. The organist must be paid! The guitarist must be paid! The sound controller must be paid and the pastor constantly seeks a higher salary for his services.

Dear friend, most of the ripened harvest fields are in the poor regions of the world. How will the poor people of the earth be reached in their poverty? Most of these people cannot pay for the services of good pastors and evangelists. The ministry of unpaid pastors and evangelists is the key to continued church planting.

Where the sacrificial nature of Christianity is compromised, church planting comes to an end. The church was born on the sacrifice of Christ. The church grew through the sacrifice of the apostolic church. Once again, the church will only expand through sacrifice.

Paul left Athens and went to Corinth, where he met Aquila, a Jewish man from Pontus. Not long before this, Aquila had come from Italy with his wife Priscilla, because Emperor Claudius had ordered the Jewish people to leave Rome. Paul went to see Aquila and Priscilla and found out that they were tent makers. PAUL WAS A TENT MAKER TOO. So he stayed with them and they worked together.

EVERY SABBATH, PAUL WENT TO THE JEWISH MEETING PLACE. He spoke to Jews and Gentiles and TRIED TO WIN THEM OVER.

Acts 18:4 (Contemporary English Version)

2. It is possible to combine secular work with the ministry.

Lay ministry requires the ability to combine secular work with real ministry. The best example of the lay ministry was the Apostle Paul's ministry. It is a ministry in which you support yourself. You may ask, "Is this the way that God planned for ministry to be?" "Does the Bible not teach that they that preach the gospel must live of the gospel?"

Even so hath the Lord ordained that they which preach the gospel should live of the gospel.

1 Corinthians 9:14

I combined being a medical student with ministry. I know many people who are effectively ministering the Word of God and continuing in their professions. Paul was the great church planter of the New Testament. He was able to accomplish great things for the Lord whilst he supported himself with the tent making business. The lay ministry is even more vital for church planting today.

3. The best New Testament example of a lay pastor is the Apostle Paul. The best Old Testament example is the Prophet Daniel.

Daniel had three jobs:

i. He was a Member of Parliament for the Babylonian Province.

> **Then the king made Daniel a great man, and gave him many great gifts, and made him ruler over the whole province of Babylon, and chief of the governors over all the wise men of Babylon.**
>
> **Daniel 2:48**

ii. He was the Second Vice President to Belshazzar.

> **Then commanded Belshazzar, and they clothed Daniel with scarlet, and put a chain of gold about his neck, and made a proclamation concerning him, that he should be the third ruler in the kingdom.**
>
> **Daniel 5:29**

iii. He was the Prime Minister during the rule of Darius.

> **It pleased Darius to set over the kingdom an hundred and twenty princes, which should be over the whole kingdom; And over these three presidents; of whom Daniel was first: that the princes might give accounts unto them, and the king should have no damage.**
>
> **Daniel 6:1-2**

4. Sometimes it is the will of God for you to be a volunteer and sometimes it is the will of God for you to be in full-time ministry.

In one breath, the right thing to do is to be fully supported by the ministry, but in another breath the right thing to do is to support yourself. It is important that we follow the leading of the Spirit at all times. Isn't it amazing that the right thing can become the wrong thing ("Anomia"), because God said so? Paul declared that he was instructed by the Lord to be both full and hungry.

> **I know both how to be abased, and I know how to abound: every where and in all things I AM INSTRUCTED BOTH TO BE FULL AND TO BE HUNGRY, both to abound and to suffer need.**
>
> **Philippians 4:12**

5. Lay pastors and volunteers will become prominent in the last days.

Paul's ministry still lives on today. The best way some people can help in the ministry is to be like Paul - secular work during the week and then "reasoning in the synagogue with the Jews on the Sabbath day".

And because he was of the same craft, he abode with them, and wrought: for by their occupation they were tentmakers. AND HE REASONED IN THE SYNAGOGUE every sabbath, and persuaded the Jews and the Greeks.

Acts 18:3-4

6. Paul practised the lay ministry so that others would follow his good example.

I now place you in God's care. Remember the messages about his great kindness! This message can help you and give you what belongs to you as God's people. I have never wanted anyone's money or clothes. You know how I HAVE WORKED WITH MY OWN HANDS TO MAKE A LIVING FOR MYSELF and my friends.

By everything I did, I showed you how you should work to help everyone who is weak. Remember that our Lord Jesus said, "More blessings come from giving than from receiving." After Paul had finished speaking, he knelt down with all of them and prayed.

Acts 20:32-36 (Contemporary English Version)

For yourselves know how ye ought to follow us: for we behaved not ourselves disorderly among you; Neither did we eat any man's bread for nought; but wrought with labour and travail night and day, that we might not be chargeable to any of you: Not because we have not power, but to make ourselves an ensample unto you to follow us.

2 Thessalonians 3:7-9

I am talking about a fruitful and lasting ministry. Paul was not a powerful church planter. It is time for many who are called to follow this good example.

7. Lay pastors and volunteers can be just as fruitful as full-time ministers.

I do not know of anyone who will say that the Apostle Paul was inferior to any of the other apostles. He laboured more abundantly and travelled more extensively. He planted more churches than any one else did. He was truly an effective, anointed and fruitful pastor.

Chapter 5

Why You Must Become a Lay Pastor

1. Become a lay pastor so that you can live in certain geographical locations and do the ministry.

When missionaries were sent from Switzerland to Ghana two hundred years ago, they had to support themselves on the mission field. Many of them became farmers, teachers etc. There was obviously no way of making bank transfers to these missionaries. It is important for ministers to understand that there are times when secular work gives you the legitimate basis for being in particular places. I have pastors in certain countries that do secular work simply because they need to be able to live in that country legally.

Are we ready to do anything for Christ Jesus our Lord? If you have to hold down a secular job so that you can live and minister in a strange land will you do it? Is that asking too much? How do you think the Prophet Daniel was able to flourish in Babylon? He maintained his job as a Member of Parliament.

2. Become a lay pastor so that you are not a burden to anyone.

Neither did we eat any man's bread for nought; but wrought with labour and travail night and day, THAT WE MIGHT NOT BE CHARGEABLE TO ANY OF YOU.

2 Thessalonians 3:8

There are times when being a full-time minister is a burden to a small congregation. Sometimes a particular person in the congregation is burdened by the fact that he has to support you all the time. There are times I wouldn't want to stay in certain people's homes. This is because I feel that my presence is burdensome to my host. Once we went out preaching and we got back home very late. It was past midnight. Our hostess came out of her room looking very sleepy and tired.

She said, "Oh, are you guys back?"

"What time is it?" she mumbled.

We found out that it was about one a.m.

"Would you like to eat?" She asked.

I thought to myself, "Of course I would like to eat. I am starving; I haven't eaten the whole day." But I muttered some non-committal and diplomatic answer.

My hostess continued, "I have some fish in the freezer, I can defrost it and make some stew."

I was quiet but she continued, "I have some rice which I can also prepare."

Then she asked again, "Would you like me to make the food?"

I thought to myself, "Should a Christian ask someone to defrost fish and boil rice at one a.m.?" I decided that I didn't want to be a burden to this dear hostess.

I smiled sheepishly and said, "Oh, it is alright."

I went to bed on an empty stomach. I simply did not want to be a burden to my hostess.

I have learnt to carry secret supplies of food with me when I travel so that I do not become a burden to people. This is what Paul was talking about. He did not want his ministry to become a burden to anyone.

3. **Become a lay pastor so that you can survive in ministry without being paid by the church.**

Neither did we eat any man's bread for nought; but wrought with labour and travail night and day, that WE MIGHT NOT BE CHARGEABLE TO ANY OF YOU:

2 Thessalonians 3:8

Four Ways That Paying a Pastor Can Hinder the Ministry

a.   Building projects are slowed down or stopped.

b.   The church cannot buy the equipment it needs.

c.   Missionaries cannot be sent out.

d.   Immature church members who do not understand why pastors should be paid certain amounts of money could cause trouble in a new church. Some people simply do not understand why people who work for God should be blessed. I advise pastors to keep their lives as private as possible.

4.   Become a lay pastor so that you are "free" from all men.

For though I be FREE FROM ALL MEN, yet have I made myself servant unto all, that I might gain the more.

1 Corinthians 9:19

Many times people who give money develop an attitude because of the size of their donations. It is very important for pastors to be free from the negative attitudes of church members. The prophets were warned, "Don't be afraid of their faces." This is because the facial expression on people's faces often intimidates us. There are times when our being lay ministers eliminates the need for people's gifts and donations hereby eliminating these bad attitudes.

For though I preach the gospel, I have nothing to glory of: for necessity is laid upon me; yea, woe is unto me, if I preach not the gospel! For if I do this thing willingly, I have a reward: but if against my will, a dispensation of the gospel is committed unto me. What is my reward then? Verily that, when I preach the gospel, I may make the gospel of Christ without charge, that I abuse not my power in the gospel.

For though I BE FREE FROM ALL MEN, yet have I made myself servant unto all, that I might gain the more.

1 Corinthians 9:16-19

5. **Be a lay pastor so that you can be in the ministry whether finances permit it or not.**

   For though I preach the gospel, I have nothing to glory of: for NECESSITY IS LAID UPON ME; yea, woe is unto me, if I preach not the gospel!

   For if I do this thing willingly, I have a reward: but if against my will, a dispensation of the gospel is committed unto me. What is my reward then? Verily that, when I preach the gospel, I may make the gospel of Christ without charge, that I abuse not my power in the gospel.

1 Corinthians 9:16-18

Paul said, "Woe is me if I preach not the gospel." Sometimes we do not have a choice! We have to do His will whether there is a salary or not.

That is exactly how I feel. I do not think that I have a choice. I am bound to obey God. I feel that if I do anything apart form preaching His Word, God will destroy me. I have heard other pastors say the same thing.

One pastor said to me, "Before I was in the ministry, I knew that God had called me. At one time I felt that God would kill me if I didn't go into the ministry."

He continued, "That is why I am in full-time ministry today."

6. **Be a lay pastor to ensure that you have a part in this great ministry.**

   For he was numbered with us, and HAD OBTAINED PART of this ministry.

Acts 1:17

Many of us may never play a part in building the kingdom unless we do it as lay people. Are all apostles? Are all prophets? Are all evangelists? Are all pastors? Obviously not! But thank God you can support yourself and make a significant contribution to the ministry as a lay pastor.

7. Be a lay pastor so that you will be able to relate better with other volunteers.

Many full-time pastors are unable to relate to lay pastors. The lay ministry is a good foundation for a pastor. Because ministers of the gospel have never practised the lay ministry, they do not encourage laymen in the church to rise up and be volunteers. God is merciful and He makes a way for all kinds of people to help in the ministry.

8. Be a lay pastor so that you can sacrifice to the Lord.

The lay ministry is essentially sacrificial in nature. Unlike what many people think, the ministry is very tiring and stressful. Even paid ministers are often called upon to sacrifice.

Many pastors do not have a normal family life because their family life is constantly interrupted by the incessant demands of the congregation. When it is holiday time, instead of the pastor having time for his family, he has to attend various church and social functions. No one really cares about it until the pastor's children become rebels.

There are many pastors' children who hate the ministry. They feel the ministry steals their parents from them. Besides this, there are many stresses that come to the pastor and his wife by virtue of the position they hold. He is the focus of every spiritual attack; many people do not know this.

One time, when Israel went to war with Syria, the Syrian king gave a very revealing command to his generals and to his captains. He said to them, "Do not fight with anyone. DON'T FIGHT WITH THE GREAT AND DON'T FIGHT WITH THE SMALL, FIGHT ONLY WITH THE KING PERSONALLY."

But the king of Syria commanded his thirty and two captains that had rule over his chariots, saying, Fight neither with small nor great, SAVE ONLY WITH THE KING OF ISRAEL.

1 Kings 22:31

You can see from this instruction that no target was significant enough except the King of Israel himself. The king represents the leader or the pastor who becomes the focus of the attack.

When a person takes on the sacrifices of ministry without being paid, he makes a double sacrifice.

Am I not an apostle? am I not free? have I not seen Jesus Christ our Lord? are not ye my work in the Lord? If I be not an apostle unto others, yet doubtless I am to you: for the seal of mine apostleship are ye in the Lord. Mine answer to them that do examine me is this, HAVE WE NOT POWER TO EAT AND TO DRINK? HAVE WE NOT POWER TO LEAD ABOUT A SISTER, A WIFE, AS WELL AS OTHER APOSTLES, AND AS THE BRETHREN OF THE LORD, AND CEPHAS? Or I only and Barnabas, have not we power to forbear working?

Who goeth a warfare any time at his own charges? who planteth a vineyard, and eateth not of the fruit thereof? OR WHO FEEDETH A FLOCK, AND EATETH NOT OF THE MILK OF THE FLOCK? Say I these things as a man? or saith not the law the same also? For it is written in the law of Moses, Thou shalt not muzzle the mouth of the ox that treadeth out the corn. Doth God take care for oxen? Or saith he it altogether for our sakes? For our sakes, no doubt, this is written: that he that ploweth should plow in hope; and that he that thresheth in hope should be partaker of his hope.

If we have sown unto you spiritual things, is it a great thing if we shall reap your carnal things? If others be partakers of this power over you, are not we rather? Nevertheless we have not used this power; but suffer all things, lest we should hinder the gospel of Christ. Do ye not know that they which minister about holy things live of the things of the temple? and they which wait at the altar are partakers with the altar? Even so hath the Lord ordained that they which preach the gospel should live of the gospel. But I have used none of these things: neither have I written these things, that it should be so done unto me: for it were better for me to die, than that any man should make my glorying void.

For though I preach the gospel, I have nothing to glory of: for necessity is laid upon me; yea, woe is unto me, if I preach not the gospel! For if I do this thing willingly, I have a reward: but if against my will, a dispensation of the gospel is committed unto me. What is my reward then? Verily that, when I preach the gospel, I may make the gospel of Christ without charge, that I abuse not my power in the gospel.

1 Corinthians 9:1-18

The lay ministry will test your Christian character. Virtues like self-control and temperance will be tested. When I was a medical student and doctor on the wards of the hospital, I had to sacrifice my resting times for the ministry. When people were watching TV, I could not afford that luxury. I didn't have time for useless socializing and chatting. All my spare time was taken up.

9. Be a lay pastor to overcome selfishness in your life.

Selfishness is the principal reason why many people do not get involved in the lay ministry. Most people are basically self-centred in their outlook of life; they have no concerns for anyone except themselves. They are engrossed in the little world they have built around themselves. Selfishness speaks of self-centredness, self-concern, self-awareness, self-help and self-gratification.

A selfish person can never be a servant of the Lord. Selfishness makes you think about yourself but ministry makes you think about people you don't even know. The Apostle Paul lamented about this phenomenon. He noted that all men seek for their own welfare.

He said, "No one cares for the things of the Lord."

For I have no man likeminded, who will naturally care for your state. For all seek their own, not the things which are Jesus Christ's.

Philippians 2:20-21

We are all selfish by nature but the deeper we get in the Lord, the less selfish we become. The barrenness of most Christians is a result of the spirit of selfishness.

Who cares if they go to Hell? At least I am going to Heaven. Who cares if there is a village somewhere that has not heard the gospel? At least my family and I are okay. Who cares if somebody is sick and lying on the hospital ward? At least I am well. Who cares if there is some dirty old prisoner languishing in jail? At least I am free!

That is the spirit of selfishness at work in the church and the Christian.

If Jesus had been selfish, He would not have left His throne in glory and come to this rotten world.

10. Become a wise lay pastor.

Behold, I send you forth as sheep in the midst of wolves: be ye therefore wise as serpents, and harmless as doves.

Matthew 10:16

Because of the intrinsic hatred for God and the ministry, many people would like to pick on someone who claims to be a pastor.

There was a man of the Pharisees, named Nicodemus, a ruler of the Jews: The same came to Jesus by night, and said unto him, Rabbi, we know that thou art a teacher

**come from God: for no man can do these miracles that
thou doest, except God be with him.**

John 3:1-2

People often look out for your faults at work or at school.
They say things like, "I am surprised that a pastor would do that.
I never knew that pastors also come to work late."

I remember when I worked at the Korle Bu Teaching Hospital,
the biggest hospital in my country, as a doctor; I never told them
I was a pastor. I knew that at the slightest opportunity they would
use it against me. While a student and a pastor, I never indicated
that I was even religious. I didn't want them to know anything
about me.

It is foolishness to go announcing to the whole world that you
are a pastor or a religious leader. Jesus said we should be as wise
as serpents. What does it mean to be as wise as a serpent? What
wisdom does the serpent have? It has the wisdom to exist quietly
in the midst of people who hate it.

The serpent is universally hated and killed on sight, with no
questions asked. And yet, snakes flourish all around us. There
are millions of snakes all over the world. How has the snake
managed to live and multiply in a world that hates it utterly? By
discretion, carefulness, judgment, secrecy, prudence and caution!

**11. Be a lay pastor so you can be a financial support to the
ministry.**

**I have shewed you all things, how that so labouring ye
ought to SUPPORT THE WEAK, and to remember the
words of the Lord Jesus, how he said, It is more blessed
to give than to receive.**

Acts 20:35

It is amazing that a large amount of financial support comes
from my lay pastors. Many times when there is a special appeal
for financial support, it is my lay pastors who often support me

most. When you are involved in the ministry; you know the needs of the ministry. Lay ministers are a good support base for every church.

12. Be a lay pastor to overcome laziness and idleness in the church.

For we hear that there are some which walk among you disorderly, working not at all, but are busybodies.

2 Thessalonians 3:11

After people have been in the church for some years, they seem to know all your sermons. No matter what tricks you use, they are able to see through the message and identify where it is coming from.

I remember preaching a powerful series in church. People were really blessed. Many commented on how powerful the services had been. Then I had a note. This note was from a long-standing church member.

He wrote, "Dear pastor we were tremendously blessed by your message tonight."

He continued, "This is exactly what you preached five years ago. You only changed the title."

He went further and enumerated the messages from where he claimed I had duplicated my current series.

Then to reassure me he said, "We were mightily blessed anyway so keep on doing the good work."

You see, it is important that Christians get involved with the ministry otherwise they become critical busy bodies, analyzing and commenting on things that they do not even understand.

LORD, my heart is not haughty, nor mine eyes lofty: neither do I exercise myself in great matters, or in things too high for me.

Psalm 131:1

Chapter 6

How I Operated as a Lay Pastor

I have experienced two worlds of ministry: full-time ministry and lay ministry. Most pastors are only aware of the existence of the full-time dimension of ministry. My intention is to help you to discover the reality of how lay people can cause the church to grow.

A lay person is someone who maintains his secular job and yet is active in the ministry of the Lord Jesus. A full-time minister is someone who has abandoned his secular job to concentrate fully on the ministry.

Many ministers who are in full-time ministry are not comfortable with the idea of lay people participating in the ministry. This is because they want to maintain the ministry as the exclusive preserve of a few "called" men of God. Some full-time ministers do not want to accept the reality that lay people are capable of making a substantial (non-financial) contribution to ministry. Many full-time ministers are happy to maintain their lay people as mere financial supporters.

Pastors want to feel special as they perform their exclusive ministerial duties. "Why should a lay person do what I do?" they say. They think, "After all, if you can do the job I'm doing, what makes me special? What makes me (the pastor) different if lay people can do the things I do?"

Many ministers are not convinced that lay people can do the work of the ministry. I have had pastors ask me, "Will they have time to attend to the needs of the flock?", and "Can they handle emergencies?" "Can they minister powerfully the way we do?" The answer to these is very simple - a resounding YES! I have been in the lay ministry for many years and have found it to be practically possible.

Churches that have experienced phenomenal growth have all employed the principle of using lay people. I believe that it is the key to fulfilling the Great Commission. There is no way we are going to win this world with a few priests and pastors. Everyone must get involved. Many people must get involved at a higher ministerial level. There must be a revival of the lay ministry in the church.

There is such a thing as a lay pastor, i.e., a pastor who combines both his secular job and does the ministry as well. Ninety percent of the pastors in my church are lay pastors.

Full-time pastors must be secure in their positions in order to encourage lay people to get involved. There is nothing mystical about the ministry! There are pastors who want the ministry to be shrouded in mystery so that their members feel dependent on them.

It is something that many can get involved with. What a blessing it is for lay people to discover that they can be useful in the ministry! What a blessing for the pastor when he discovers that the contributions of lay people can make his church grow. I am not saying that there is no need for full-time ministers. I am myself a full-time minister. There is a great need for full-time ministers to be one hundred percent involved in ministry work. There are things that only full-time ministers can do.

I Was a Lay Pastor

At the age of about fifteen, in secondary school, I met the Lord. From the day I gave my life to Christ, I became very active in ministry. I was involved in soul winning and following up converts. I was also involved in singing and playing musical instruments for the Lord.

In the first phase of my Christian life, I was not a traditional Sunday morning church attendee. In fact, I hardly went to church on Sundays. My Christian life was so active from Monday to Saturday that I ended up resting on Sundays! On Mondays and Wednesdays I had a prayer meeting and Bible study. On Tuesdays and Thursdays I had music rehearsals. On Fridays we had fasting and prayer meetings. And then on Saturdays we would have a retreat from ten in the morning until six in the evening.

Whilst I was involved in these activities I did not give up my schooling. I completed my GCE 'O' levels and passed with a distinction - I had seven ones (one is the highest mark of distinction). That was a great accomplishment by any standards. In my GCE 'A' levels I topped my class and was one of only three people from my school admitted into the medical school. Throughout this period, I was fully involved in ministry. I preached! I won souls! I visited people in their homes! I counselled many people! I fasted and prayed! At one point, I fasted so much that I became as thin as a rake. Someone even asked me, "Do you think that you will get to Heaven by being a skeleton?"

Never did it occur to me that I had to be paid for the ministry work that I was involved in. By the time I was nineteen years old, I was fully involved in the ministry. I had many sheep who looked up to me for direction and prayer. By 1980, I was a strong preacher and leader of the Scripture Union fellowship. The point I am making is that ministry is possible alongside other pursuits. I entered the university in October 1982. I was privileged to be studying medicine - one of the most difficult and time-consuming courses. Whilst in the university I began a Christian fellowship that is still in existence today.

During my fourth year, I began to establish the foundations for a church. I then became a pastor and was acknowledged as such whilst I was still a medical student. During this time I was not being paid by anyone to do the work of the ministry. Neither did I slacken in my academic work. On the contrary, I did extremely well and won prizes in the medical school. I applied wisdom and sacrificed my leisure time so that I could be involved in ministry.

Sacrifice and Wisdom

These are the two keys to being in the lay ministry - *sacrifice and wisdom*. What is the main task of a pastor? Is it to perform funerals and to officiate weddings? Certainly not! These are certainly duties of a minister but they are not main duties. If your ministry has deteriorated to the point where your main functions are to conduct marriages and bury people, then you need to read your Bible again! The main duty of a minister is to fulfil the Great Commission.

Go ye therefore, and teach all nations, baptizing them in the name of the Father, and of the Son, and of the Holy Ghost: Teaching them to observe all things whatsoever I have commanded you: and, lo, I am with you alway, even unto the end of the world. Amen.

Matthew 28:19, 20

The reason why it is called the Great Commission is because it is the great commandment to all ministers. It is sad to see ministers of the Gospel who have become mere social functionaries. Sometimes pastors are under pressure to be accepted by society. As a result, they want to do nice things that relate to health, education, etc., so that they may gain the approval of society.

Apostle Peter came under the same pressure to leave his principal duties and to perform mainly social tasks.

And in those days, when the number of the disciples was multiplied, there arose a murmuring of the Grecians against the Hebrews, because their widows were neglected in the daily ministration.

Then the twelve called the multitude of the disciples unto them, and said, It is not reason that we should leave the word of God, and serve tables.

Wherefore, brethren, look ye out among you seven men of honest report, full of the Holy Ghost and wisdom, whom we may appoint over this business.

BUT WE WILL GIVE OURSELVES CONTINUALLY TO PRAYER, AND TO THE MINISTRY OF THE WORD.

Acts 6:1-4

You can see from this Scripture that Peter's main duty was to pray and to minister the Word. This is something that can be done by lay people.

Lay people can be taught to visit and counsel younger Christians!

Lay people can be taught how to preach!

Lay people can be taught how to witness!

Lay people can be taught how to minister the Word with power!

Lay people can be taught to make spiritual gains through prayer!

What I have just described is the work of a pastor. Any honest reader will agree that a lay person can become a lay pastor.

What you need is a systematic way of training your lay people to become ministers. Do not limit your lay people because they are professionals in other fields. Do not say that your doctors, lawyers, architects, carpenters, engineers, tailors, masons, nurses and secretaries, cannot be pastors. They can!!

I remember visiting one of our churches that was pastored by a female nurse. There were hundreds of people in the church and I gave glory to God for that. In a large house there are many vessels. God is using all kinds of people. Do not limit God to what you have been used to.

But in a great house there are not only vessels of gold and of silver, but also of wood and of earth; and some to honour, and some to dishonour. If a man therefore purge himself from these, he shall be a vessel unto honour, sanctified, and meet for the master's use, and prepared unto every good work.

2 Timothy 2:20-21

When I was in my first year at the university, I was told by the Christian fellowship that *I could not be a leader because I was a medical student.* Medical students were considered too busy to be involved in ministry work. How unfortunate! They had effectively eliminated a whole group of potential leaders from the fellowship.

This is what many pastors do. They look at the doctors in the church and think to themselves, "Sit down quietly, receive your Sunday sermons and pay your tithes. Be a nice principled Christian doctor who does not perform abortions and you will please God!!"

I want you to know that a doctor can also please God by winning souls. It is true that God wants principled doctors. But God also wants doctors who will win souls and do the work of ministry. Today, I have doctors who own clinics and at the same time pastor churches with hundreds of members.

There are many architects who do full-time architectural work and are very fruitful in ministry. There are pastors who work in banks but pastor large churches. I have seen teachers, pharmacists, university lecturers, accountants, students, doctors, nurses, army officers, civil servants, air conditioner repairers, computer scientists, computer technicians, businessmen, and lawyers become great lay pastors. Many people cannot believe that our long lists of pastors are lay people who are not paid by the church.

If pastors understand that their *lay people can do much more than just give money* to the church, they would help themselves and their churches a great deal. That is what this section is about - showing how lay people can help the church to grow.

Please do not misunderstand me; not every lay person must become a pastor. Some of the lay people can function as ordinary shepherds (cell leaders). But there are others who have the call of God upon their lives and who will become pastors.

The Pineapple Patch

One day as I was walking on a hillside I saw something that I want to share with you. I was praying in tongues and walking along a footpath on one of the hills in Ghana. The entire hillside was covered with wild bushes and tall untamed grass. As I walked along, I saw a section within the wild grass measuring about

20 meters by 20 meters. In that particular section there were neatly planted pineapple plants. I could see the baby pineapples sprouting. That section of the hillside was very different from everywhere else.

The Spirit of the Lord spoke to me and said, "That section of the hillside is different because certain seeds have been planted there. That area of the hillside is different because some special investment has been made on that patch of ground." The Lord told me that the rest of the hillside can be likened to the general congregation which receives seeds of normal preaching. The special patch of ground that was yielding pineapples could be likened to the part of the church that received the special seeds of leadership and pastoral training.

If you sow the seeds of pastoral training you will soon have many more pastors and leaders around you.

Many people do not invest the seeds that give rise to leaders, pastors and shepherds. If you sow the seeds that train leaders, you will harvest a crop of well-seasoned leaders. I spend more time with my leaders than I do with the general congregation. The teachings in this book are examples of some of the things I have taught ordinary people over the years.

This investment has turned many people into shepherds and lay pastors! Invest specially in leaders and potential pastors and they will grow up to become great ministers!

I have heard people criticizing me for starting churches with people whom they consider not to be pastors. Do not criticize someone who has been holding Shepherds' Camps to train people. Criticize yourself for not having spent hours training your own lay people to be in the ministry.

You must encourage your lay people to become something more than principled citizens of the country. You must encourage them to become soul winners for Jesus. You must want them to be shepherds of God's flock. You must want them to fulfil the Great Commission.

Dear pastor friend, I wrote this book for you! God told me to write it so that you will understand that lay people can and will help you to build your church.

God has a ministry for you. Please do not go to Heaven and discover that you did not even begin your ministry! Take what you are reading seriously and learn the art of shepherding and pastoring. Discover for yourself the joy of serving God as a layman.

Chapter 7

How to Share the Burden with Lay People

And the Lord said unto Moses, Gather unto me seventy men of the elders of Israel, whom thou knowest to be the elders of the people, and officers over them; and bring them unto the tabernacle of the congregation, that they may stand there with thee. And I will come down and talk with thee there: and I will take of the spirit which is upon thee, and will put it upon them; and they shall BEAR THE BURDEN of the people with thee, that thou bear it not thyself alone.

Numbers 11:16, 17

One of the most difficult tasks in life is to "lead" people. Moses delivered the Israelites from bondage but struggled to lead them to the Promised Land. They were too difficult for him to handle. Moses' job of leading difficult people is the job that all pastors have to do.

God graciously gave Moses spectacular and sensational miracles. These signs and wonders helped to establish his authority over God's flock. In spite of this, the burden of leading the people was more than he could carry. The Bible calls it a burden - and that is what it is! Moses eventually succumbed to the pressures of leading difficult people and lost his chance to enter the Promised Land.

There Is a Real Burden

If you have a pastor's heart and love people, you cannot disassociate yourself from their problems. Their problems will become your problems and their burdens will affect you! When God uses you to minister to a large number of people, he expects you to share the burden. Failure to share this burden simply means that you may collapse or come to a standstill in ministry. There are many standstill churches around. They grow to a point but can grow no further. The reason is that they fail to share the burden of ministry.

A balanced church is one that has people of all sorts within it; young, old, educated and uneducated, rich and poor, and male and female. All these people must be drafted in to the share the burden.

Don't Exclude Anyone

I notice that most churches exclude the educated and the rich from ministry. Usually, the rich are expected to contribute money whilst the educated enhance the image of the church. However, I have found that both the rich and the educated can be spiritually useful. There are many medical doctors, carpenters, plumbers, specialists, lecturers, architects, and engineers, who serve as lay pastors. These lay pastors share the burden of ministry.

The burden of the ministry cannot be borne by one person. It is simply impossible.

Share the Burden and Have a Larger Church

If you want to have a greater ministry than what you currently have, you must share the burden. Sometimes people do not share the burden because they want to take all of the glory for themselves. They want people to feel that they are the only ones with a supernatural gift. They want people to show appreciation to them alone.

Others are afraid of rebellion in the camp. How common is the story of associate pastors rebelling. Many senior pastors fear their assistants will outshine them one day. Fear not, only believe! You cannot expand without trusting people. The work is so great that you will never ever be able to do it all alone.

1. Lay people will help you deal with ungrateful and forgetful sheep.

...in the last days... men shall be... unthankful...

2 Timothy 3:1-2

There will always be lay people who are very grateful for your ministry. They will love you and appreciate your efforts for them. These people will help to neutralize the presumption that is common in the congregation. Their grateful speeches will neutralize rebellion in the camp.

You will notice ungratefulness in people by the way they complain. Moses led the Israelites out of bondage and slavery and yet they murmured and complained bitterly against him. Aaron even had to make a golden calf to calm them down. If something ever goes wrong, you will be surprised at the reactions of people you have ministered to. Many quickly forget what you have done for them. The things a pastor does are not physically tangible, but spiritual. Many therefore think that the pastor has done nothing for them.

Church members can sin against you after you have been a blessing to them. Don't be shocked! The prophet Jeremiah experienced the same thing from his people. He said, "Shall evil be recompensed for good?" (Jeremiah 18:20).

The Sin of Hezekiah

Once, a pastor told a very disturbing story. He said that he was surprised when one of his church members came to his house one night to assault him. He couldn't believe that this young man whom he had led to Christ, trained up in the Lord, whose marriage he had blessed, and helped through various crises would attack him in that manner.

Dear friend, do not be surprised! Do not expect gratitude from man; expect your rewards from God. Hezekiah was blessed. But he did not "render again". That means he did not show gratitude for all the blessings he had received.

But Hezekiah RENDERED NOT AGAIN according to the benefit done unto him...

2 Chronicles 32:25

This is the nature of man. This is the nature of the people God wants you to lead.

2. Lay people will help you overcome disloyalty in the congregation.

With the help of lay people, you will be able to fight disloyalty in the church. The presence of zealously committed lay workers always inspires more loyalty in the ranks. Lay people, who do not earn money from the church, are a great support to every pastor. Lay people who are loyal will report what is going on in the congregation.

Though Judas walked and ministered with Jesus for three years, he eventually betrayed him for a small amount of money. Betrayal is a part of ministry. It is also a part of life. If you have yet to experience betrayal, I can assure you that you will. The disturbing thing about betrayal is that it comes from people who are supposedly close to you.

You are not greater than your master Jesus! The fact that someone may betray you one day makes it very difficult for you to happily interact and flow with the people. Look closely at the ministry of any great man of God. You will discover that they have all had their fair share of traitors. All of this contributes to the burden and difficulty of ministry.

Yea, mine own familiar friend, in whom I trusted, which did eat of my bread, hath lifted up his heel against me.

Psalm 41:9

Paul experienced sudden desertions by some of his colleagues, like Demas. I remember one young man whom I trained. He was about to take up an important position in the ministry that we had been preparing for, for over a year. On the day he was to fill the position, he suddenly informed me that he was leaving the country. I couldn't believe my ears! All of our months of preparation meant nothing to him. He just abandoned ship without notice. These experiences are all part of the ministry. Abandonment also occurred under the ministry of Apostle Paul.

For Demas hath forsaken me...

2 Timothy 4:10

Because people can abandon you at any time, it is burdensome to lead them. The presence of committed lay people will always help to share the burden of abandonment. God wants us to be involved in His work. God wants us to be shepherds!

3. Lay people will help to deal with disrespectful and rebellious church members.

And Miriam and Aaron spake against Moses... Hath the Lord indeed spoken only by Moses? HATH HE NOT SPOKEN ALSO BY US?

Numbers 12:1-2

There are lay people who will sort out disrespectful and rebellious church members for you. You always need people on the ground to deal with church members who make light of pastors. There are people who think their money and status in the secular world gives them a right to say and do anything in the church.

Miriam and Aaron (the closest assistants and closest relatives) spoke against Moses. They most probably said things like, "God also speaks by us" and "Are you the only one God uses?" With time, familiarity creeps in and arrogant people now consider you as an equal. They tend to think, "We can all do it. What's the big deal? You are no different from us!"

This is unfortunate, but real. People easily take you for granted. They murmur and complain against you, forgetting all that you have done for them. When some church members lose their temper, they will speak to you as though you are a little child.

"You Remind Me of My Father"

One church member approached her pastor after Sunday service. The pastor thought she was about to compliment him for the powerful sermon he had just preached.

She started, "Pastor, you know something? I felt I should tell you that you remind me of my father."

"Oh really?" the pastor responded. He thought he reminded her of some good traits in her father.

She continued, "He was so full of himself and so are you!"

The pastor was taken aback but had to smile and continue as though he had received a compliment. This church member was telling the pastor exactly what she thought of him. Moses also experienced rebels who thought he was "too big" for his shoes. Moses also had people who wanted to cut him down to size. That is why Moses had to share the burden with seventy other elders.

Now Korah... and Dathan... and Abiram... and On... rose up before Moses... and said... wherefore then lift ye up yourselves [Moses and Aaron] above the congregation of the Lord?

Numbers 16:1-3

4. Good lay people encourage others to respond positively to the Word.

When any one heareth the word of the kingdom, and UNDERSTANDETH IT NOT...

Matthew 13:19

The domino effect is when one thing leads to another. When one lay person responds positively to your teaching, others are inspired to do the same. It is always a blessing to have ordinary congregants who are outspoken in their support of you. Sometimes large sections of the congregation do not understand the Word.

Often they do not understand why you have to do fundraising. Consequently, many do not respond in giving. Many times, I have to explain that they are giving to build a nice church where they can have their weddings, their baby dedications and their ceremonies.

Leading people who have all the above characteristics: ungratefulness, disloyalty, etc., is a major task. One person cannot do it alone. The burden must be shared with others. Sharing the burden is hard work.

5. Lay people will cause the church to expand by becoming part of the workforce.

The use of lay people as part of the workforce is the secret to unlimited expansion of the church.

Sometimes people think that lay people cannot do much ministry work. Do not be deceived - try using lay people and you will discover how much work they can do.

Lay people can join the pastors to share the burden of the people. Let your lay people know that they are called to share the burden of ministry with you. They will share the burden on earth and they will share the burden of accounting for the sheep in Heaven.

When we established churches in the universities, we entrusted the preaching and pastoring responsibilities to students. I am very proud of these student ministers because of the great job that they have done on the different campuses. I don't have to rush to the different universities every Sunday morning to minister the Word. Ordinary saints have joined in to help.

These saints must be perfected (prepared, trained) to do the work of the ministry. Ordinary saints can do the work.

For the perfecting of the saints, for the work of the ministry, for the edifying of the body of Christ:

Ephesians 4:12

The principal strategy for distributing the burden is to involve lay men and women in ministry. No church is capable of employing an endless number of people. Every church has a limit to its resources.

It is not possible to pay salaries and rent an unlimited number of houses for the staff of the ministry. Full-time staff are limited in the amount of work that they can do.

6. Lay people will help you with prayer, visitation, counselling and interaction.

Lay people can help you with the burden of praying, visiting, counselling and interacting with the sheep.

Moses was breaking down under the burden of having to pray, visit, counsel and interact with so many people. God saw a disaster waiting to happen and decided to take of the "spirit" that was on Moses and put it on the seventy leaders "to bear the burden" with him.

And the Lord said unto Moses, Gather unto me SEVENTY MEN of the elders of Israel... THAT THEY MAY STAND [work] THERE WITH THEE.

Numbers 11:16

Involving students, workers, and professionals helps to distribute the burden to all saints in the church. The Lord wants everyone to be fruitful no matter what they do in life.

7. Lay people will help you to account for the sheep on the Day of Judgment.

...for they watch for your souls, AS THEY THAT MUST GIVE ACCOUNT, that they may do it with joy...

Hebrews 13:17

The burden of answering for the sheep cannot be borne by one person or a few people who supposedly have a "call". The burden of accounting for hundreds of different people cannot be borne by one person. When I stand before the judgment seat and God asks me about certain souls, I intend to refer to the lay pastors and shepherds I put in charge of these souls.

When the Lord asks me about some souls in the church, I intend to find out who was in charge and tell the Lord to ask that person. I cannot possibly answer for all these different people personally.

Every pastor will have a lot to answer for when he stands before the Lord in Heaven. Your burden is to be able to lead all your sheep to Heaven. Make sure you lose none of them. Every pastor must hope to say, "Of all that you have given me, I have lost none!" Jesus said this phrase in three different places – John 6:39, John 17:12; and John 18:9.

Chapter 8

The Ideal Lay Pastor

1. The ideal lay pastor is a volunteer for life. He does not turn aside from his commitment to volunteer himself to the ministry. The best lay pastors are those who give themselves to the lay ministry for life. They do not waver from their initial commitment.

2. The ideal lay pastor is a good shepherd and a good pastor. He has learnt how to be a good shepherd and how to care for the sheep.

3. The ideal lay pastor is a good businessman or professional. He has learnt how to flourish in his chosen secular profession or business. Most of the lay pastors who become rebellious have financial problems and are tempted to use the ministry as an additional source of income.

4. The ideal lay pastor is good at combining the pastoral work with secular work. He has overcome all the difficulties and challenges of combining these two very different activities.

5. The ideal lay pastor has a great respect for full-time ministry, even though he himself does not leave his secular profession for the ministry. The ability to genuinely respect full-time priests, even though you are not entering it yourself, is a mark of the ideal lay pastor.

6. The ideal lay pastor is sacrificial. The ideal lay pastor will give up much of his rest and leisure time for the ministry.

7. The ideal lay pastor is loyal and persistent in ministry, even through the mid-life crises of his life. Non-ideal lay pastors fall away during their mid-life crises and during their financial dry seasons.

Chapter 9

What Is the Proper Attitude of
a Lay Pastor?

Render therefore to all their dues: tribute to whom tribute is due; custom to whom custom; fear to whom fear; honour to whom honour.

Romans 13:7

The right attitude for a lay pastor is to respect the full-time ministry! Great honour is due men who have given up everything to be in the ministry. The secular world may not respect the office of a priest. Non-believers may have no regard for the work of a full-time minister. But a lay pastor must definitely have the greatest respect and understanding for the work of a full-time pastor.

The right attitude for a lay pastor is to respect full-time ministry. To be a successful volunteer or lay pastor, you must have the right heart and the right attitude towards real ministry. If you do not respect full-time ministry you will not walk in the full anointing of your calling.

How a Lay Pastor Can Prove His Respect for Full-Time Ministry

1. **A lay pastor proves his respect for full-time ministry when he is not non-committal on the subject of full-time ministry.** Some lay people and volunteers say little or nothing when it comes to the subject of full-time ministry. Their silence on this subject reveals hidden misgivings about the need for people to be in full-time ministry. Indeed, a lay pastor must have a clear and positive attitude towards full-time ministry.

2. **A lay pastor proves his respect for full-time ministry when he honestly admits that he does not have the courage or boldness to be in full-time ministry.** The reality is that many lay pastors were afraid to take the bold step of entering into full-time ministry and that is why they are still lay pastors. An honest admission of this weakness will deliver them from dishonesty, untruths and continuing self-deception. When you admit that you were afraid to enter into full-time ministry, you honestly admit that full-time ministry is a great thing and only great people are able to enter it.

3. **A lay pastor proves his respect for full-time ministry when he speaks highly of full-time ministry.** Words of honour and words of respect for the priesthood and those who have entered it reveal your utmost respect for full-time ministry.

4. **A lay pastor proves his respect for full-time ministry when he is able to encourage others to be in full-time ministry even though he is not.** A healthy respect for full-time ministry is revealed when you are able to encour-age others to do something that you were unable to do. When outsiders support people who are in ministry, it reveals a deep-seated love and respect for the ministry. Hannah showed her support for her son's ministry by making a coat for him every year.

But Samuel ministered before the Lord, being a child, girded with a linen ephod.

Moreover his mother made him A LITTLE COAT, and brought it to him FROM YEAR TO YEAR, when she came up with her husband to offer the yearly sacrifice.

1 Samuel 2:18-19

5. **A lay pastor proves his respect for full-time ministry when he is able to defer to and receive counsel from a full-time pastor.** A lay pastor can show his respect and esteem for full-time ministry by deferring to full-time ministers. The ability to receive counsel from a person fully dedicated to ministry is a sign of respect for the ministry. Unfortunately,

some lay people despise full-time ministers, thinking that they have no knowledge or input to make in secular life and work. Because they obviously despise the ministry, they are kept away from committing themselves to the profession.

Chapter 10

Double-Minded Lay Pastors

You must make up your mind about whether to be a layperson or to go all out into ministry. A double-minded man is unstable in all his ways. The last thing you must be double-minded about is your career! You cannot be double-minded about your ministry! Are you in full-time ministry or in lay ministry? Which is your calling? Choose you this day whom you will serve!

Evil Effects of Double-Mindedness on the Ministry

1. **Double-mindedness about lay and full-time ministries introduces instability into your life.** When a layperson is undecided about what he is doing, he is uncertain as to whether he should go all out in his secular ambitions or he should give himself to ministry.

   A double minded man is UNSTABLE in all his ways.

   James 1:8

2. **Double-mindedness about lay and full-time ministry reveals a lack of honesty and truth.** You must be truthful to yourself. You must not deceive yourself about what your calling is. If God has called you to the ministry, then give yourself to that cause. Do not wait until you see financial opportunities before you switch from lay ministry to full-time ministry. Which side do you belong to? What is your calling? Be truthful to yourself about who you are and about what God wants you to do. When the belt of truth is loose, you open yourself up to corrupt thoughts of wickedness.

Draw nigh to God, and he will draw nigh to you. Cleanse your hands, ye sinners; and PURIFY YOUR HEARTS, YE DOUBLE MINDED.

James 4:8

3. **Double-mindedness about lay and full-time ministries exposes you to a love-hate relationship with the ministry.** You cannot serve mammon and God. In a sense, full-time ministry represents serving God whilst lay ministry represents serving mammon.

In lay ministry, your principal job is to do with secular work, whereas in full-time ministry your principal job is to do with the church. Many lay men and volunteers are double-minded and end up either loving the ministry and hating their secular jobs or hating the ministry and loving their secular jobs. Make up your mind today! Be a lay preacher for life or be a full-time preacher for life! You cannot serve two masters. You must choose who will be your master.

No servant can serve two masters: for either he will hate the one, and love the other; or else he will hold to the one, and despise the other. Ye cannot serve God and mammon.

Luke 16:13

4. **Double-mindedness about lay and full-time ministries introduces a long period of confusion into your life and ministry.** Confusion is the fruit of double-mindedness. God is not the author of confusion. You must decide where you belong. How long will you waver between two opinions? People who have wavered between two opinions have ended up neither prospering in the secular world nor flourishing in the ministry.

And Elijah came unto all the people, and said, HOW LONG halt ye between two opinions? If the Lord be God, follow him: but if Baal, then follow him. And the people answered him not a word.

1 Kings 18:21

And if it seem evil unto you to serve the Lord, CHOOSE YOU THIS DAY whom ye will serve; whether the gods which your fathers served that were on the other side of the flood, or the gods of the Amorites, in whose land ye dwell: but as for me and my house, we will serve the Lord.

Joshua 24:15

5. **Double-mindedness about lay and full-time ministries is a demonstration of immaturity.** Your ability to choose something and to stick to your choice reveals maturity. This is why certain jobs are only given to people who are married. Marriage reveals a person's ability to choose one of many options that are available to him.

Immature flighty young men cannot make up their minds! But the mature person will decide on one person and stay with his choice. Indeed, it is maturity that enables a person to choose either the lay ministry or full-time ministry for the rest of his life.

That we henceforth be no more CHILDREN, TOSSED TO AND FRO, and carried about with every wind of doctrine, by the sleight of men, and cunning craftiness, whereby they lie in wait to deceive;

Ephesians 4:14

6. **Double-mindedness about lay and full-time ministries will cause you to have a faulty ministry.** I have observed many faulty ministers who have wavered between lay ministry and full-time ministry for many years. God is calling you to make up your mind and do what is right. If God has given you one talent, make the most of it and be a good lay minister. If God has given you ten talents, make the most of it and be a good full-time minister.

THEIR HEART IS DIVIDED; NOW SHALL THEY BE FOUND FAULTY: he shall break down their altars, he shall spoil their images.

Hosea 10:2

Chapter 11

Understanding How Lay Ministry Is a Measure of Ministry

1. **Lay ministry is a measure of ministry.** Indeed, every one of us has only a measure of ministry. Jesus is the only one who was given the ministry without a measure. "For he whom God hath sent speaketh the words of God: for God giveth not the Spirit by measure unto him" (John 3:34). Jesus Christ is the only one whose ministry was not limited. He did not receive a portion. Everybody has been given a measure of a gift. A lay pastor is a measure of the pastoral gift.

2. **Lay people have the grace of God for their measure of ministry.** Everyone has grace for what he is called to do. Some people wonder how a medical doctor can also pastor a church. Some people are surprised that an accountant can run a church. Where do they find the time to do the work? How can they study and prepare? Will the church ever be able to grow? Indeed, laymen can help the church to grow. God uses laymen to do great things. They are able to accomplish great things because of the grace that is upon their lives. A full-time pastor may not have that grace and may have to prepare much more to be able to run his church.

But unto every one of us is given GRACE ACCORDING TO THE MEASURE of the gift of Christ.

Ephesians 4:7

3. **Lay people must not think of themselves more highly than they ought to.** The lay ministry is a small measure of ministry. No matter how long you have been a lay pastor, you are still only a lay pastor. You are not a professional priest who is dedicated to the things of God. You have been granted grace to operate as a lay minister. It is the grace of God that allows lay people to be part of this wonderful ministry.

For I say, through the grace given unto me, to every man that is among you, NOT TO THINK OF HIMSELF MORE HIGHLY THAN HE OUGHT to think; but to think soberly, according as God hath dealt to every man the measure of faith.

Romans 12:3

4. **Lay people must not exalt themselves above full-time ministry.** You must not boast of things that are outside your measure. You must accept the measure you have been given. A lay pastor must not exalt himself above a full-time minister. A lay pastor must be humble in the presence of someone who is fully dedicated to the ministry. In the same way, when a full-time pastor visits the workplace of the lay pastor, he will accord the lay pastor the necessary respect in his chosen profession.

When lay pastors begin to think they are what they are not, the church suffers loss. I have seen churches that are hijacked by laymen who feel they are as good as full-time dedicated pastors. As a result, the church suffers decline and full-time ministry is despised. Can you imagine a bank that is run by laymen who work elsewhere and visit the bank at weekends and on some evenings? What would be the hope of that bank?

NOT BOASTING OF THINGS WITHOUT OUR MEASURE, that is, of other men's labours; but having hope, when your faith is increased, that we shall be enlarged by you according to our rule abundantly,

2 Corinthians 10:15

5. **Lay people should assess their ministry by the things they have suffered.** Lay people protect themselves from suffering, sacrifice and loss by maintaining their jobs in the secular world. How did Paul assess his ministry? How did he know that he was a minister of Christ? Was it by the size of his church? Was it by how old he was? Or was it by how much money he had? Indeed, it was by the things he had

suffered and endured in the ministry. When a person gives himself into full-time ministry, he risks having a lifetime of poverty and suffering. He will go through many difficulties which a lay person shields himself from through his secular career.

Lay people achieve great things for themselves in the secular world. Lay people protect themselves from suffering, sacrifice and loss by maintaining their jobs in the secular world. This is the principal difference between a lay pastor and a full-time minister of Christ. This is why Paul revealed his true rank by the things that he suffered and not by the things he had achieved.

Are they ministers of Christ? (I speak as a fool) I am more; in labours more abundant, in stripes above measure, in prisons more frequent, in deaths oft.

Of the Jews five times received I forty stripes save one.

Thrice was I beaten with rods, once was I stoned, thrice I suffered shipwreck, a night and a day I have been in the deep;

In journeyings often, in perils of waters, in perils of robbers, in perils by mine own countrymen, in perils by the heathen, in perils in the city, in perils in the wilderness, in perils in the sea, in perils among false brethren;

In weariness and painfulness, in watchings often, in hunger and thirst, in fastings often, in cold and nakedness. . . .

The God and Father of our Lord Jesus Christ, which is blessed for evermore, knoweth that I lie not.

In Damascus the governor under Aretas the king kept the city of the Damascenes with a garrison, desirous to apprehend me: And through a window in a basket was I let down by the wall, and escaped his hands.

2 Corinthians 11:23-27, 31-33

Chapter 12

Understanding How Lay Ministry Is a Type of Helps Ministry

And God hath set some in the church, first apostles, secondarily prophets, thirdly teachers, after that miracles, then gifts of healings, HELPS, governments, diversities of tongues.

1 Corinthians 12:28

Lay ministry is simply another form of the helps ministry. The main line of work in the church is the ministry of apostles, pastors, teachers, evangelists and prophets. There are, however, people who are called to help these principal ministers of the body of Christ.

The word, helps comes from a Greek word antilepsis which means *"to aid, to participate, to support, to relieve* and *to assist"*. In a sense, the helps ministry is a vague, limitless and undefined ministry. Help is not easy to define and it can take almost any form. There are many things that are helpful and so anything that is helpful can be considered as the helps ministry.

The Bible has several examples of helps ministers and these examples help to reveal what a true helps minister is. Indeed, lay ministry is one of the largest sections of helps ministry. An unpaid lay person can assist an apostle, prophet, teacher or apostle in many different ways. A lay person can assist by preaching the Word of God. A lay person can assist by doing administrative work. A lay person can assist by caring for and supporting a minister of God.

When someone does any of these things without charge he is a layman in the helps ministry.

Examples of Helps Ministers

1. Onesiphorus the helps minister of Paul

But God bless Onesiphorus and his family! Many's the time I've been refreshed in that house. And he wasn't embarrassed a bit that I was in jail. The first thing he did when he got to Rome was look me up.

May God on the last day treat him as well as he treated me. And then there was all the help he provided in Ephesus – but you know that better than I.

2 Timothy 1:16-18 (The Message)

2. The seventy lay elders, the helps ministers of Moses

These seventy elders were to help him in his pastoral care of the people of Israel. Laymen also help in the pastoral care of the flock of God. The seventy elders were lay people who were not part of the priesthood.

And the LORD said unto Moses, Gather unto me seventy men of the elders of Israel, whom thou knowest to be the elders of the people, and officers over them; and bring them unto the tabernacle of the congregation, that they may stand there with thee.

And I will come down and talk with thee there: and I will take of the spirit which is upon thee, and will put it upon them; and they shall bear the burden of the people with thee, that thou bear it not thyself alone.

Numbers 11:16-17

3. The seventy, helps ministers of Jesus' evangelistic ministry

Jesus was assisted by the seventy elders whom He sent out to prepare the way for His evangelistic campaign. Every evangelist needs forerunners who will prepare the way for the big campaign that is coming up.

After these things the Lord appointed other seventy also, and sent them two and two before his face into every city and place, whither he himself would come.

Therefore said he unto them, The harvest truly is great, but the labourers are few: pray ye therefore the Lord of the harvest, that he would send forth labourers into his harvest.

Luke 10:1-2

4. **Priscilla and Aquila, helps ministers of Paul**

Greet Priscilla and Aquila my helpers in Christ Jesus:

Romans 16:3

5. **Urbane**

Salute Urbane, our helper in Christ, and Stachys my beloved.

Romans 16:9

Chapter 13

Understanding the Deficiencies of Lay Ministry

So you shall appoint Aaron and his sons that they may keep their priesthood, but THE LAYMAN WHO COMES NEAR SHALL BE PUT TO DEATH.

Numbers 3:10 (NASB)

1. **The lay ministry is deficient because it lacks the full consecration of a Levite.**

   The full consecration that was required of Levites can never be given by a lay pastor. A study of the Bible reveals the extent to which priests had to be consecrated to God and to the ministry.

2. **The lay ministry is deficient because lay pastors do not wholly belong to the Lord.** The Levites are the Lord's. When you work at the bank, there is a sense in which the bank owns you. The bank tells you when to come to work and when to go home. These are simply realities of life.

   And I, behold, I have taken the Levites from among the children of Israel instead of all the firstborn that openeth the matrix among the children of Israel: therefore THE LEVITES SHALL BE MINE;

   Numbers 3:12

3. **The lay ministry is deficient because lay pastors cannot and do not take care of the tabernacle in the way Levites do.** Lay pastors are busy taking care of the business of the bank and other secular institutions that they work for.

   But the Levites shall pitch round about the tabernacle of testimony, that there be no wrath upon the congregation of the children of Israel: and the LEVITES SHALL KEEP THE CHARGE OF THE TABERNACLE of testimony.

Numbers 1:53

4. **The lay ministry is deficient because lay pastors do have an inheritance in the world.** The inheritance of lay pastors is their jobs. Real pastors do not have an inheritance in the world. They are wholly dedicated to the Lord and all their hope is in the Lord.

But the tithes of the children of Israel, which they offer as an heave offering unto the Lord, I have given to the Levites to inherit: therefore I have said unto them, AMONG THE CHILDREN OF ISRAEL THEY SHALL HAVE NO INHERITANCE.

Numbers 18:24

5. **The lay ministry is deficient because lay pastors do not have the time to assist the high priest in many of his duties.** Lay pastors will be at their secular jobs when needed by the high priest. A real Levite is wholly given to the work of ministry.

You shall thus give the Levites to Aaron and to his sons; THEY ARE WHOLLY GIVEN TO HIM from among the sons of Israel.

Numbers 3:9 (NASB)

6. **The lay ministry is deficient because only real Levites are fit to do the work of the priesthood.** Lay men were not allowed to approach these holy tasks.

So you shall appoint Aaron and his sons that they may keep their priesthood, but THE LAYMAN WHO COMES NEAR SHALL BE PUT TO DEATH.

Numbers 3:10 (NASB)

7. **The lay ministry is deficient because lay pastors cannot give the hours necessary for quality work.** The hours spent on your profession logically define who you are.

61

The amount of time necessary for quality fruits and results can never be provided by a part-time input. The curse of Adam requires several hours of input and sweat for any good results. Quality time must be spent on quality work. It is only in sorrow and hard work that our work on earth will yield fruits.

> And unto Adam he said, Because thou hast hearkened unto the voice of thy wife, and hast eaten of the tree, of which I commanded thee, saying, Thou shalt not eat of it: cursed is the ground for thy sake; in sorrow shalt thou eat of it all the days of thy life;
>
> Thorns also and thistles shall it bring forth to thee; and thou shalt eat the herb of the field;
>
> In the sweat of thy face shalt thou eat bread, till thou return unto the ground; for out of it wast thou taken: for dust thou art, and unto dust shalt thou return.
>
> Genesis 3:17-19

8. **The lay ministry is deficient because it is not God's ordained purpose and plan.** God's purpose is the plan that must be pursued and not our ideas. His ordained method is for His priests to work and to live off their work and be sustained by it. Lay people are not paid or sustained by the ministry. They earn money from the secular jobs they do. God's ordained plan is full-time ministry. Read the Scriptures for yourself!

> Do ye not know that they which minister about holy things live of the things of the temple? and they which wait at the altar are partakers with the altar?
>
> Even so HATH THE LORD ORDAINED that they which preach the gospel should live of the gospel.
>
> 1 Corinthians 9:13-14

9. **The lay ministry is deficient because in the lay ministry, God does not have the first honoured position that He deserves.** God will never accept to be secondary to anything or to anyone. The honoured position which God deserves is the first position; that which comes before everything else.

His work comes before the work of the bank, the work of the university, the work of private companies or even the work of the government. Everyone who works for God after working for mammon has placed God in second position. God is aware of this reality. Yet out of grace and mercy, He receives those who still want to do something for His sake.

But seek ye first the kingdom of God, and his righteousness; and all these things shall be added unto you.

Matthew 6:33

10. **The lay ministry is deficient because lay people are unable to make full proof of their ministry.** Because a lay person cannot fully perform certain duties, he cannot make full proof of his ministry. His ministry can never develop to its ultimate level of fruitfulness.

But watch thou in all things, endure afflictions, do the work of an evangelist, MAKE FULL PROOF OF THY MINISTRY.

2 Timothy 4:5

… fully perform all the duties of your ministry.

2 Timothy 4:5 (AMP)

… do a thorough job …

2 Timothy 4:5 (Message)

Chapter 14

Understanding Why God Allows Lay Ministry to Exist

1. Lay ministry comes about because of a deceptive response from those called to the work.

We all know that lay ministry is not the God-ordained kind of ministry. So why does God allow the lay ministry to carry on? When those who promised to go do not go, God is forced to fall back on lay people and even on women. Read it for yourself!

> But what think ye? A certain man had two sons; and he came to the first, and said, Son, go work to day in my vineyard. He answered and said, I will not: but afterward he repented, and went. And he came to the second, and said likewise. And he answered and said, I go, sir: AND WENT NOT.
>
> Matthew 21:28-30

2. The lay ministry came about because of a lack of labourers.

There is a genuine lack of labourers for the work of God. If you were Almighty God and you needed to save seven billion dying souls from going to Hell, would you not raise up lay men to help in this unbelievable, gargantuan harvest?

> But when he saw the multitudes, he was moved with compassion on them, because they fainted, and were scattered abroad, as sheep having no shepherd.
>
> Then saith he unto his disciples, the harvest truly is plenteous, but the LABOURERS ARE FEW;
>
> Pray ye therefore the Lord of the harvest, that he will send forth labourers into his harvest.
>
> Matthew 9:36-38

3. The lay ministry came about because of the great need.

There is a great need in the church for labourers, pastors and evangelists. Paul said, "Necessity is laid on me!" I have to do it! I need to go! Perhaps the great needs that exist in the church have forced the lay ministry to become an important arm of ministry today.

For though I preach the gospel, I have nothing to glory of: for NECESSITY IS LAID UPON ME; yea, woe is unto me, if I preach not the gospel!

1 Corinthians 9:16

4. The lay ministry came about because of people's inability to pay for true ministry.

Many times the church is unable to pay a good pastor to look after the people. Many small congregations do not have the money or resources to look after their shepherd. This results in pastors preaching and teaching the Word of God without being paid. The apostle Paul was a good example of someone who kept preaching the Word without charging for it.

For ye remember, brethren, our labour and travail: for labouring night and day, because we would not be chargeable unto any of you, we preached unto you the gospel of God.

1 Thessalonians 2:9

Chapter 15

Develop the Four Essential Skills of a Lay Pastor

A lay pastor must develop four essential skills. Just as there are four engines that power a jumbo jet, there are four engines that power up a lay pastor's life and ministry. In this chapter, I want you to think about these four essential skills that make a lay pastor complete.

1. Pastoral skills

A lay pastor must develop himself as a good pastor. He must be a good shepherd and lead the flock of God as though he were in full-time ministry. People under his care must experience the love of God and enjoy the richness of the Word of God that he preaches.

2. Business and professional skills

If the lay pastor is a businessman, he must develop very good business skills. These business skills will cause him to prosper and be successful in his business. It is dangerous to have a lay pastor who is a failure in his business. It will make him desperate and begin to have an evil eye towards the ministry.

Such people blame the ministry for their failures in business. If you are a professional such as a lawyer or a doctor, you must excel in your chosen profession. You must get to the highest possible rank that you can and become an example to other laymen. Once again, when you do not prosper in your profession, you begin to have an evil eye towards the ministry. Lay pastors who became corrupt were often failures in their chosen professions or business. In their poverty and desperation they turned on the church for financial relief.

3. Flourishing skills

A lay pastor must also develop himself in the art of flourishing. This is the art of becoming rich and prosperous. There are many people who develop themselves in their businesses or professions but are unable to convert it into real prosperity. It is important to use the art of leadership and the art of strategic thinking to help yourself to flourish. We all know many doctors and lawyers who don't have much money. They are professionals alright, but they have not flourished and do not have much money to spend. We all know many lecturers who live from hand to mouth. They are professors alright and they did earn their PhD's from famous universities. But many of these highly educated men have simply not learnt the art of flourishing.

A lay pastor must flourish; otherwise, in his midlife he will turn against the ministry he has loved and blame the church for his difficulties. Midlife crisis that begins from around the age of forty, causes men to re-evaluate all they have been involved in. Unfortunately, many laymen begin to blame the ministry for their poor performance at work and their poor flourishing skills.

A flourishing lay pastor must have an income that is far more than his expenses. A flourishing lay pastor must be able to give larger and larger amounts to the ministry.

4. Early retirement skills

A lay pastor must have early retirement skills. Perhaps the most important of these four is the early retirement skills. These skills are important to a lay pastor because as he goes forward, he is likely to want to give himself more to the work of the Lord. However, if he has not developed early retirement skills, he will be unable to retire from his secular work. He will need to go to the clinic every day and earn his living.

If a lay pastor cannot take long periods off from work, to give himself to God's work he will not be able to retire soon from his secular work. If, however, he has been successful in investing in real estate or other income-generating projects, he will be able to retire early from secular work and give himself to ministry. A lay pastor with early retirement skills will have ensured that he is genuinely free from debts and lives in his own house. Indeed, a lay pastor with early retirement skills is able to stay away from work longer and longer until one day he never has to return!

Chapter 16

The Struggles of Lay Pastors

1. Lay pastors struggle with the concept of full-time ministry.

Lest there be any fornicator, or PROFANE PERSON, as Esau, who for one morsel of meat sold his birthright.

Hebrews 12:16

A lot of lay pastors struggle with the concept of full-time ministry. However, a good lay pastor should be able to preach about full-time ministry. To despise the concept of full dedication to the house of the Lord is a mistake of grandiose proportions. Esau profaned and despised sacred things and was rejected by God. Lay pastors must not despise the concept of full-time ministry. Indeed, there must be no struggle to acknowledge the importance and validity of full-time ministry.

2. Lay pastors struggle with independence.

Many lay pastors struggle with obedience and conformity. Obedience becomes difficult as pride increases in your heart. Through disobedience and non-conformity, the spirit of independence develops. But God did not design us to be independent beings. It is obvious that we have not recognised what being independent really is. When Satan tempted Adam and Eve, an offer for independence was made to them (which is the same offer made to each of us today). Satan offered independence when he said, "You will be like God; you will not need God."

All men have this inherent struggle with independence. The seed of Satan leads the drive to independence, even when it is self-destructive. Men have more of a drive for independence than women. Research has shown that women remain faithfully in their jobs once they are treated well. Women are not as likely to change jobs as men are. On the average, men change their jobs about seven times in their lifetime.

A great difference between human beings and the rest of creation is our desire to be independent from God. Unlike the rest of the creation, human beings are always struggling to be independent of God who created them. Similarly, people who were birthed into a ministry struggle to be independent of the person who birthed them. The stars are not independent! God numbers the stars and calls them by name.

He telleth the number of the stars; he calleth them all by their names.

Psalm 147:4

The lions look to God for their food. The lions have never desired independence from God.

The young lions roar after their prey, and seek their meat from God.

Psalm 104:21

The birds and beasts look to God for their food. They have never gone away from their creator. Human beings have forsaken God and put Him out of our minds.

He giveth to the beast his food, and to the young ravens which cry.

Psalm 147:9

Jesus told us how the Father feeds the birds of the air:

Behold the fowls of the air: for they sow not, neither do they reap, nor gather into barns; yet YOUR HEAVENLY FATHER FEEDETH THEM.

Matthew 6:26

Whilst all of creation looks to God for their food, we (human beings) rather become more independent of God. Human beings are alone in their desire and pursuit of independence.

O Lord, how manifold are thy works! in wisdom hast thou made them all: the earth is full of thy riches. So is this great and wide sea, wherein are things creeping innumerable, both small and great beasts.

There go the ships: there is that leviathan, whom thou hast made to play therein.These wait ALL UPON THEE; that THOU MAYEST GIVE THEM THEIR MEAT in due season.

Psalm 104:24-27

Our struggle to be independent from God has always resulted in confusion. When you struggle to be independent from the ministry that gave birth to you, you may be motivated by Satan. Satan is the salesman of independence.

Beware! The desire for independence is not a new thing. Adam was offered this independence and he took it, landing the whole universe in utter confusion. A lay pastor must not become independent of the source of his authority.

Some lay pastors quickly become independent when they are appointed to the ministry. They feel they know everything and disconnect spiritually from the source of their spiritual existence. They no longer listen to messages or advice from their spiritual father. What a tragedy! The appointment to the pastoral office often destroys people.

3. Lay pastors struggle with keeping rank.

Lay pastors must stay in line and try not to move out of their position. The lay ministry is a layman's ministry. It is not "real" ministry and people who are practising the lay ministry must acknowledge who they are and who they are not. That is what it means to keep rank! When I drive to any court of law, I am not acknowledged as a professional lawyer even though I have written a few contracts in my lifetime. I am a lay person as far as the law profession is concerned and I have to accept that. I must stay within my rank and not think of myself more highly than I ought to.

Of Zebulun, such as went forth to battle, expert in war, with all instruments of war, FIFTY THOUSAND, WHICH COULD KEEP RANK: they were not of double heart.

1 Chronicles 12:33

4. Lay pastors struggle with offences from transfers.

Then Joab arose, and came to Absalom unto his house, and said unto him, Wherefore have thy servants set my field on fire?

And Absalom answered Joab, Behold, I sent unto thee, saying, Come hither, that I may send thee to the king, to say, Wherefore am I come from Geshur? IT HAD BEEN GOOD FOR ME TO HAVE BEEN THERE STILL: now therefore let me see the king's face; and if there be any iniquity in me, let him kill me.

2 Samuel 14:31-32

Absalom was transferred to Geshur. On his return he wanted to live in the same house as the king. He reacted angrily when the king would not see him.

People who struggle with being transferred from place to place are often agitated by spirits of rebellion. Just like Absalom, they do not want to be where they are placed.

Lay pastors are support staff in ministry and ought not to struggle with any kind of transfers. Pride makes a lay pastor offended with a transfer. It is pride that makes a pastor resign because he has been transferred. A lay person must accept that he is a helper to those who are in full-time ministry. He cannot dictate what must be done and how the church must be run. I know several lay pastors who were greatly offended when they were asked to move and serve in another capacity.

5. Lay pastors struggle with corrections and rebukes.

Reprove not a scorner, lest he hate thee: rebuke a wise man, and he will love thee.

Proverbs 9:8

A pastor must not be angry when he is rebuked. He must receive correction like a child who is humble and open. Unfortunately, some lay pastors are puffed up because of their long service. After some years in lay ministry, they consider themselves too big to be corrected or rebuked. Such "big" pastors must be shown the exit sign and made to leave. Their continued presence in the ministry will pollute younger ones and the leaven of pride and rebellion will spread. There is no place for these "big" men in the work of the Lord.

6. Lay pastors struggle with delegated authorities.

... He that believeth on me, believeth not on me, but on him that sent me.

John 12:44

Lay pastors must receive delegated authorities with joy. As the church grows larger, people you do not know will be appointed and may have authority over you. The air hostess on a plane may not know who the pilot is but she has to respect his rank as the commander of the aircraft. It is the rank and the appointment that she must respect. In the same way, lay pastors must receive and accept people who are appointed over them. Failure to accept delegated authority is a recipe for anarchy and confusion in the ministry. How is it that a lay pastor can accept authority in his secular job but reject authority in the church world? Away with these rebels! Let them leave the house of the Lord for those who are humble enough to accept delegated authorities.

7. Lay pastors struggle with combining their secular life with ministry.

Lay pastors struggle to combine secular work with ministry. This is a struggle that will always be there. Indeed, it is not easy to handle two completely different jobs and be successful at both. It takes the grace of God. But that is what lay ministry is all about. There are many people who have successfully combined secular work with their spiritual work. God will bless them for the sacrifices they have made.

Beside those things that are without, that which cometh upon me daily, the care of all the churches.

2 Corinthians 11:28

8. Lay pastors struggle with the transition into full-time ministry.

Verily, verily, I say unto you, He that entereth not by the door into the fold of the sheep, but climbeth up some other way, the same is a thief and a robber.

John 10:1

There is a proper way to enter full-time ministry. Without humility, lay pastors are unable to bow down and go through the entrance door to priesthood. To come into full-time ministry involves giving up everything and sacrificing yourself for the ministry. Transitioning into full-time ministry is not the same as getting an alternative job. The ministry is not an alternative to secular work. It is a calling that must be entered into soberly, advisedly and with lowliness of mind.

The transition to full-time ministry is not the grasping at an alternative source of income. Sadly, some lay pastors begin to see the church as a source of income. When these lay pastors were offered the opportunity to work for the Lord, they rejected it because they thought they would lose everything by working for God. When they began to see the possibility of earning money from the ministry, they suddenly changed their minds about lay ministry and grasped at full-time ministry with their greedy hands.

Why did they not give themselves to the ministry when they were young, fresh, energetic and intelligent? Why did they wait until they were having a midlife crisis and in need of additional income to pay their children's university fees? Do they now look upon the church as a source of money which can cater for their needs? No, no, no! The ministry is not a business and the ministry must not be entered because of your need for money. That is not the legitimate door to ministry. You must enter into ministry in obedience to the call of God. You must enter into ministry because it is the will of God. You must enter into ministry because you love God and because you desire to please Him. Above all, you must enter full-time ministry because God has called you to do so.

9. Lay pastors struggle with closeness.

> Draw nigh to God, and he will draw nigh to you. Cleanse your hands, ye sinners; and purify your hearts, ye double minded.
>
> James 4:8

Lay pastors struggle to stay close to the anointing which they need. It is important to draw near and stay near. Being close is both an art and an act of humility. Pride creates a gap and brings the aloofness that is so common in some lay pastors and volunteers. They stand at a distance and stare as though they are not welcome. Guilt keeps them away when indeed they should be close by, helping in the ministry.

Don't stand far away! You are loved! You are wanted! You are needed! Come closer and be as involved as you can.

10. Lay pastors struggle with pride.

> Be of the same mind one toward another. Mind not high things, but condescend to men of low estate. Be not wise in your own conceits.
>
> **Romans 12:16**

Pride comes from being around for a long time. Sometimes, pride grows in lay pastors when they pastor a successful church. Pride is also seen in pastors who have churches in rich cities. Pride also filters into the lives of lay pastors when they are successful at their secular work.

You must overcome the temptation of the pride that comes by being an opinion leader and a prominent person. Korah is a perfect example of a lay pastor who went berserk because of his position in society. Success in the secular world must not destroy a lay pastor! Korah's outrageous demands to Moses are recorded in the Bible. Korah was a layman who challenged the holiness of Moses, telling him off and informing him that he was not the only holy person who could pray to God. Watch out Mr. Layman!

> Now Korah, the son of Izhar, the son of Kohath, the son of Levi, and Dathan and Abiram, the sons of Eliab, and On, the son of Peleth, sons of Reuben, took men:
>
> And they rose up before Moses, with certain of the children of Israel, two hundred and fifty princes of the assembly, famous in the congregation, men of renown:
>
> And they gathered themselves together against Moses and against Aaron, and said unto them, Ye take too much upon you, seeing all the congregation are holy, every one of them, and the Lord is among them: wherefore then lift ye up yourselves above the congregation of the Lord? ...
>
> And Moses said unto Korah, Hear now, ye sons of Levi: Seemeth it but a small thing unto you, that the God of Israel hath separated you from the congregation of Israel, to bring you near to himself, to do the service of the tabernacle of Jehovah, and to stand before the congregation to minister unto them;
>
> And that he hath brought thee near, and all thy brethren the sons of Levi with thee? And seek ye the priesthood also?
>
> Numbers 16: 1-2, 8-10

11. Lay pastors struggle with hypocrisy.

Hypocrisy involves appearing to be more committed and righteous than you really are. Ananias and Sapphira suffered from this. They pretended that they were giving more than they actually did. But there is no need to pretend to be more committed, more sacrificial and more spiritual that you really are.

Some lay pastors constantly pretend that they want to be in full-time ministry. All through their lives, they pledge, they promise and they affirm that full-time ministry is all that they want to do with their lives. Like Ananias and Sapphira, they make commitments they cannot keep.

They present themselves as being more zealous and more committed than they really are. Relax my brother and be yourself! Not everyone has been called to full-time ministry! It is not a sin to be a lay pastor! It is a privilege! It is an honour and it is a great thing that you are a lay pastor.

Do not live your life pledging to be somebody you cannot be. Be happy with what God has made you and rejoice in your portion of the lay ministry. **Do not live a life of unnecessary guilt!** God is happy with your contribution to the ministry.

> But a certain man named Ananias, with Sapphira his wife, sold a possession, And kept back part of the price, his wife also being privy to it, and brought a certain part, and laid it at the apostles 'feet.

> But Peter said, Ananias, why hath Satan filled thine heart to lie to the Holy Ghost, and to keep back part of the price of the land? Whiles it remained, was it not thine own? and after it was sold, was it not in thine own power? why hast thou conceived this thing in thine heart? thou hast not lied unto men, but unto God.

Acts 5:1-4

12. Lay pastors struggle with deceptions and delusions.

> And with all deceivableness of unrighteousness in them that perish; because they received not the love of the truth, that they might be saved.

2 Thessalonians 2:10

Why Lay Pastors Struggle with Delusions

a. **Lay pastors struggle with delusions because they use the same titles and uniforms as full-time ministers.**

Lay pastors struggle with deception. It is easy to believe you are something that you are not. The roots of the deception of lay pastors lies in their using the same titles and sometimes wearing the same uniforms as full-time ministers. There are lay pastors of small churches who use the title "General Overseer" whilst some founders of huge denominations are also called General Overseers. Such use of similar titles leads to deceptions about who a lay pastor really is. Many laymen wear a collar whilst full-time priests also wear a similar collar. Of course, they are deceived into thinking that they are priests of the same rank. But this is not the case!

A lay person wearing a collar has been given the privilege to share in the ministry that the few full-time pastors can never fulfil on their own.

b. **Lay pastors struggle with delusions because they engage in the same activities as full-time ministers.**

Delusions also come to lay pastors because they engage in the same activities as full-time ministers. Lay pastors often preach as much as full-time ministers. The ability of laymen to officiate weddings and funerals leaves them with the delusion that they are equal to full-time priests and pastors. What they do not realise is that they are simply helping the full-time pastors to carry out some of their many tasks.

c. **Lay pastors struggle with delusions because they receive appreciation and offerings from church members.**

Delusions abound even more when lay pastors receive offerings from church members. When lay pastors receive letters of love and appreciation from their church members, they feel appreciated for their ministry efforts. At their secular work place, no one writes letters of love to the lay pastor and no one gives him love offerings. All these offerings can establish delusions in a lay pastor until he thinks he is as good as a full-time priest. It is important that a lay pastor continually affirms that he is simply a helper of a full-time priest.

d. **Lay pastors struggle with delusions because they minister under the covering, good name and calling of a large ministry.**

Deceptions and delusions come when people minister under the momentum and good name of a large ministry. Usually, the covering of an apostle's call provides the momentum for lay pastors to function. It is unfortunate that these lay pastors would begin to think that they themselves are apostles.

Lay pastors, guard yourselves from delusions! I have seen many lay pastors fall flat on their faces as they dived out of their God-given covering.

13. Lay pastors struggle with endurance.

Therefore, my beloved brethren, be ye stedfast, unmoveable, always abounding in the work of the Lord, forasmuch as ye know that your labour is not in vain in the Lord.

1 Corinthians 15:58

Lay pastors struggle with endurance. A lay pastor must be steadfast, unmoveable, always abounding in the work of the Lord. Many lay pastors give up ministry in their midlife. But you must survive the tests of a lay pastor and persist in the lay ministry. A lay pastor must continue ministering through his middle age, through the midlife crisis zone and into retirement.

Midlife crisis is a syndrome which many people go through. In their midlife beginning from the age of forty, people begin to experience certain well-known symptoms. These are: 1) A search for an undefined dream or goal. 2) A deep sense of regret for goals not accomplished. 3) A fear of humiliation among more successful colleagues.

Indeed, this problem peaks at about the age of forty-six. Many people in this age group experience these symptoms and struggle with the desire to do something new and different. But what new and different thing can you do apart from serving the Lord faithfully? A spiritual person cannot be led by midlife crises. You must overcome the midlife crisis. You must endure to the end. Endurance is a key characteristic of a true spiritual pilgrim.

Chapter 17

The Example-Setting Ministry
of Volunteers

1. Volunteers are an example of zeal.

A volunteer is an example of someone zealous for the Lord. Without the zeal of the Lord you will not be able to combine secular work and ministry. When I was a medical student, I needed extra zeal to add any non-medical activities to my life. Indeed, it took the zeal of the Lord to start a church through witnessing and door-to-door evangelism. Every step of the lay ministry was a step of great zeal and faith in the Lord.

> For I know the forwardness of your mind, for which I boast of you to them of Macedonia, that Achaia was ready a year ago; and YOUR ZEAL HATH PROVOKED VERY MANY.
>
> 2 Corinthians 9:2

2. Volunteers are an example of hard work.

A volunteer sets the example of hard work. It is hard work to preach and teach the Word of God and at the same time do your secular duties. A lazy person can never be a successful lay pastor. Many lay pastors are exhausted and weary after a day of this combined effort.

> And I have been a constant example of how you can help those in need by working hard. You should remember the words of the Lord Jesus: 'It is more blessed to give than to receive.'
>
> Acts 20:35 (NLT)

3. Volunteers are an example of Christ-likeness that others can follow.

Volunteers are an example of Christ. Jesus Christ gave up His life and had no thought for His own well-being. He gave His everything to fulfil the will of His father. Today, every step you take in lay ministry is a step towards being like Jesus Christ the Saviour. I honour lay pastors because they are a good example of Jesus Christ. May God increase the number of lay pastors and volunteers in our churches so that the sacrificial character of Jesus Christ will be evident to all!

Be ye followers of me, even as I also am of Christ.

1 Corinthians 11:1

4. Volunteers are an example of a pattern of good works.

Lay pastors reveal a pattern of good works. Without being paid they give off everything they have, expecting their reward from Heaven. This pattern of sacrifice reveals real Christian virtues that can be emulated by the rest of the church. I pity any minister who does not have lay pastors and volunteers eagerly working around in the church.

In all things SHEWING THYSELF A PATTERN OF GOOD WORKS: in doctrine shewing uncorruptness, gravity, sincerity,

Titus 2:7

5. Volunteers are an example to be remembered in a good way, even if dead.

I have officiated a number of funerals of lay pastors. Indeed, in their death, their works speak and testify of how fruitful and sacrificial they were in their lifetime. Today, on our Wall of Remembrance are the names of lay pastors who laid down their lives to build the church. Without the contribution of lay pastors and volunteers, a church will never experience a certain level of fruitfulness.

By faith Abel offered unto God a more excellent sacrifice than Cain, by which he obtained witness that he was righteous, God testifying of his gifts: and by it he being dead yet speaketh.

Hebrews 11:4

Chapter 18

Why We Must Fight to Protect the Lay Ministry

There is good news for laymen! I have good news for all volunteers who perform their services willingly and without pay. The message that laymen can have a part in this great work is truly good news for those who love God but are unable to give themselves wholly to this calling. This good news is that in a large house, there are many vessels. God is able to use different kinds of vessels to do His work. He can use volunteer vessels and He can use dedicated full-time priests.

You must not allow anyone to destroy this wonderful provision that the Lord has made. It is important that you do not pervert the concept of lay people being in the ministry. The lay ministry must remain pure and must continue as unpaid volunteer work. When the lay ministry is corrupted, volunteers want to be paid and begin to ask for money. Corrupted lay pastors want to be paid for their volunteer services and begin to grasp after benefits.

The leader of a large denomination once lamented about the lay preachers in his denomination who were demanding cross-country vehicles to be given to them on their retirement from the lay ministry. They demanded money and benefits that are reserved for people who do the ministry on a full-time basis. Obviously, the concept of lay ministry was corrupted and changing into something totally different from what it started as.

Every church that has embraced the lay ministry must fight to preserve it. There will always be people who start out as volunteers but metamorphose into hawks who want to be paid for everything they do. When people realise that the church is not as poor as they thought, they see their lay ministry as an alternative job and want to get as much as they can out of it.

Fight the Enemies of Lay Ministry

1. Do not allow people to corrupt the good news that lay people can also work for the Lord.

As we said before, so say I now again, if any man preach any other gospel unto you than that ye have received, let him be accursed.

Galatians 1:9

Paul was sure of what he was teaching. He believed in the gospel being sent to the ends of the world free of charge. Freely have you received, freely give. That is the gospel that we preach. Do not give place to people who turn the ministry into a business. No not even for an hour! "To whom we gave place by subjection, no, not for an hour; that the truth of the gospel might continue with you" (Galatians 2:5). The absence of lay people working for God is a tragedy. The absence of volunteers in a church is a mistake. Everybody can do something for God. If everyone has to be paid for every little thing he does, what hope is there for the church? We are standing in the midst of seven billion souls who need to find Jesus Christ before it is too late. To remove lay people and volunteers is to remove a large section of God's working force. Let us resist all those who corrupt the lay ministry and destroy the army of the Lord from within.

2. Openly oppose those who corrupt the purity of the ministry.

But when I saw that they walked not uprightly according to the truth of the gospel, I SAID UNTO PETER BEFORE THEM ALL, If thou, being a Jew, livest after the manner of Gentiles, and not as do the Jews, why compellest thou the Gentiles to live as do the Jews?

Galatians 2:14

Paul opposed Peter when he walked in hypocrisy. He rejected the very scent of corruption as it tried to enter the ministry. We must also reject those who corrupt the ministry! The ministry can be corrupted from many angles, including from the laymen. The lay ministry can be destroyed by those who no longer want to sacrifice themselves for the ministry. If we allow this, there will be no more volunteers in the ministry. Without lay people, most of the world will not be reached and the gospel will be hindered.

3. Do not build the lay ministry and destroy it afterwards.

For if I BUILD AGAIN THE THINGS WHICH I DESTROYED, I make myself a transgressor.

Galatians 2:18

It is madness to build up an army of volunteers and then destroy it by killing the culture of self-sacrifice. Churches that have worked with lay people must always value them, even when full-time workers become prominent. It is madness to promote lay ministry and later destroy it because you have some new ideas.

4. Do not frustrate the grace of God that works through lay people.

I DO NOT FRUSTRATE THE GRACE OF GOD: for if righteousness come by the law, then Christ is dead in vain.

Galatians 2:21

When lay people are able to grow a church as though they were full-time priests, it is because of the grace of God. The grace of God helps the layman to do things as though he is in full-time ministry. Through the grace of God, a lay person may minister as though he was a prophet, an apostle, an evangelist, a teacher or a pastor. When the grace of God is at work, a person is supernaturally lifted up.

Unfortunately, some lay people take the grace of God for granted and begin to think that being in full-time ministry is not necessary. They feel that they, as laymen, have been able to accomplish just as much as full-time ministers. They do not realise that it is God who has worked supernaturally to enable them do certain things.

Some lay people who are helped so much by the grace of God begin to think they are even better than full-time priests because they are not paid by the church.

5. Do not allow witchcraft in the church to manipulate and corrupt the truth about lay ministry.

O foolish Galatians, WHO HATH BEWITCHED YOU, that ye should NOT OBEY THE TRUTH, before whose eyes Jesus Christ hath been evidently set forth, crucified among you?

Galatians 3:1

People who operate in witchcraft try to manipulate the truth and cast a slur on lay ministry. They attack full-time ministers and say that full-time ministers enjoy benefits while they work for nothing. Such words corrupt the sacrifice of ministry and stir up people to think that they are being cheated.

People who once sacrificed their lives happily in the service of the Lord, begin to have an evil eye towards the ministry and no longer want to sacrifice or pay the price. Watch out for witchcraft that prevents people from obeying the truth of God's Word. As Paul said, "I am afraid of you, lest I have bestowed upon you labour in vain." Indeed, such people must be feared because they can wipe out the entire volunteer force that is needed to work in the ministry. I remember a lay pastor who wrote a letter to me with a calculation of how many miles his car had driven as he did pastoral work. He wanted the church to pay for his car because of the mileage it had accrued. How sad it is when laymen begin to calculate their sacrifices and present a bill to the Lord.

6. Fight for the birth of the lay ministry.

My little children, of whom I TRAVAIL in birth again until Christ be formed in you.

Galatians 4:19

Paul was fighting for Christ to be formed in the church of Galatia. What did Paul mean by that?

Paul wanted the character of Christ to be formed in the people who had been born again. What is the character of Christ? It is the character of humility, obedience and self-sacrifice. Such traits do not come to people easily. Such traits do not enter a church easily! A church can easily have a vampire culture in which everyone wants to drink the finances of the church of Jesus Christ. In the vampire culture, no one does anything for free. To change such a culture, you must fight with all your might.

You must travail in birth until the sacrificial and humble character of Christ is formed in your church. You must fight to have an army of volunteers in the church. It is not easy to introduce the culture of sacrifice and volunteer service to a church. In today's world, everybody wants to be paid. If you fight for this culture, it will successfully be birthed into the church.

7. Cut off the little leaven that will leaven the whole lump.

A little leaven leaveneth the whole lump.

Galatians 5:9

You must remove people who do not understand what it means to be a lay pastor. You must urgently eliminate those who are not prepared to sacrifice. If you have instrumentalists who are not prepared to play instruments without being paid, get rid of them.

If you have even one musician or talented singer who charges a fee for his services, you must get rid of that person urgently. He will pollute the rest of them and no one will be happy to work for the Lord free of charge.

If you have a lay pastor who begins to eye the offering, you must get rid of him. Volunteers must not think about the money that the church receives. A volunteer is there to work for the Lord without charge. If a volunteer wishes to give himself wholly to the ministry, he is welcome to the ministry. But he must not come to the ministry because he sees it as an opportunity to earn some money.

8. Do not be weary of lay ministry.

And let us not be weary in well doing: for in due season we shall reap, if we faint not. As we have therefore opportunity, let us do good unto all men, especially unto them who are of the household of faith.

Galatians 6:9-10

Unfortunately, many volunteers say to themselves, "I've had enough of the church. I cannot continue to spend my time and money serving for nothing." But lay pastors and volunteers must not become tired of the sacrifices they make. The rewards of ministry are great. God has huge harvests waiting for those who have sown the seeds of personal sacrifice and humility. It must be a joy to take up every opportunity that presents itself to lay people. If you are a lawyer, you must be overjoyed that there is a case you can do for the church without charging. If you are an accountant, you must be overjoyed that there are some accounts you can do for the church without charging a fee. What a blessing it is to do something for the Lord!

I noticed how people who became lay pastors in their twenties became weary of the ministry in their forties. Weariness and discouragement had set in! But we must not be weary of well doing. We must continue to work for the King of kings to the very end.

And further, by these, my son, be admonished: of making many books there is no end...

Ecclesiastes 12:12

Books by
Dag Heward-Mills

V00005BC/7/P